Think Less; Do More:

Create An Action Bias, Stop Overthinking, and Learn How to Actually Change Your Life

By Peter Hollins,

Author and Researcher at petehollins.com

Table of Contents

PART 1: THE ACTION MINDSET — 9

CHAPTER 1: LOWER YOUR STANDARDS—YES, REALLY! — 11

REMIND YOURSELF THAT ALL YOUR ATTEMPTS HAVE VALUE — 15
FORGET PERFECTION — 17
FOCUS ON PROCESS, NOT OUTCOME — 18
JUST START — 19
GO WITH WHAT WORKS — 22

CHAPTER 2: ACTION IS THE BEGINNING OF MOTIVATION — 25

ACTION CREATES MOTIVATION CREATES COMMITMENT — 31

PART 2: WHAT DOES SUCCESS REALLY TAKE? — 41

CHAPTER 3: GET COMFORTABLE WITH RISK — 41

IT'S NORMAL TO FEEL FEAR — 44
HOW TO TAKE SMART RISKS — 48

CHAPTER 4: UNDERSTANDING THE FOUR LEVELS OF ACTION — 55

WHAT MASSIVE ACTION LOOKS LIKE — 63

CHAPTER 5: HOW TO OVERCOME RESISTANCE: EXTERNALIZE IT — 71

Two Ways to Overcome Resistance — 75

PART 3: LEARNING TO SAY YES, LEARNING TO SAY NO — 89

CHAPTER 6: ONE TRICK TO DOUBLE YOUR CHANCE OF SUCCESS: IMPLEMENTATION INTENTION — 89

You Don't Need Willpower, Just a Plan — 94
How to Use Implementation Intentions to Act — 95

CHAPTER 7: MAKE A NOT-TO-DO LIST — 101

Decide What You DON'T Care About — 104

CHAPTER 8: FIND YOUR PRIORITIES — 113

The "Burner List" — 113
Warren Buffett's 5/25 rule — 117

PART 4: GETTING ORGANIZED — 127

CHAPTER 9: SIMPLIFY YOUR DECISION-MAKING WITH A SUPERSTRUCTURE METHOD — 127

Step 1: What is your intention? — 131
Step 2: What is each task's value? — 133
Step 3: What does each task cost? — 136

STEP 4: NOW SCHEDULE YOUR TASKS	137

CHAPTER 10: DAVID ALLEN'S GTD—"GETTING THINGS DONE" 141

ACTION LISTS	151
AN EXAMPLE	154

PART 5: OVERCOMING THE ROADBLOCKS 161

CHAPTER 11: HOW TO USE THE CHARACTER ALARMS METHOD 161

CHAPTER 12: BEAT PROCRASTINATION WITH MICROTASKS 171

WHEN NOT TO USE MICROTASKS	178
FOCUS ON FLOW	181

CHAPTER 13: WORK WITH YOUR ULTRADIAN RHYTHMS 185

CAN'T YOU OVERRIDE YOUR CYCLES?	190
WHAT IF MY JOB SETS MY SCHEDULE FOR ME?	191
WHEN YOU WORK, WORK; WHEN YOU REST, REST	193

SUMMARY GUIDE 199

Part 1: The Action Mindset

In the quest for a more organized, more productive, and more fulfilling life, there's certainly no shortage of advice out there. But **there is one key feature that separates those strategies that work from those that never do: action.**

It doesn't matter whether you're trying to improve your family life or relationships, achieve your career goals, improve your health, or pursue some other meaningful life goal. **At some point, if you truly wish to transform your life, you will need to cross over from where you are to where you want to be—by taking action**.

In the chapters that follow, we'll explore what it really takes to perform in the top one percent of people and to achieve your dreams. We'll see that a "bias toward" action is the single most powerful mindset to cultivate, since it's this that will keep you focused, effective, and clear. There are many myths that may be holding you back. For example, the belief that

- You need to strive for excellence at all times

- You need to constantly find ways to motivate yourself
- To be like super successful people, you need to learn to banish fear and be completely confident...

But what if you knew that none of this was required for genuinely transforming your life? In this book, we'll be looking at the single factor that has the power to move you forward in life, and how to develop it every single day. We'll turn conventional wisdom upside down and learn effective ways to prioritize, make decisions, beat procrastination, get organized, and start taking real risks that bring real rewards. Let's dive in!

Chapter 1: Lower Your Standards—Yes, Really!

"If it's worth doing, it's worth doing well."

Have you ever heard this? Perhaps you were one of those people who grew up with a parent telling you this. On its face, this advice seems sound—inspiring, even. Try your best, do things as brilliantly as you can, and don't let yourself get away with half measures and lukewarm effort. Wouldn't it be great to hold yourself to high standards this way, to strive for excellence, and to apply yourself fully to your endeavors?

Well, of course it would. But consider the unspoken part of this advice: "If it's worth doing, it's worth doing well . . . *or else don't bother.*"

To begin cultivating a mindset that favors action, we need to dig deep and unroot all those attitudes and beliefs that are actually working against us. Let's say you really did follow this advice and told yourself that it was **excellence or nothing**. You would do things properly or not at all. So you try, and guess what? Your first attempt is a little lackluster. Because you're a beginner, you don't get it done perfectly. Perhaps you fail outright. You set the bar high and then don't meet it. You look at your decidedly un-excellent performance, conclude that it's worthless, and obviously give up.

Giving up is the natural conclusion from advice that seemed so reasonable at first. If you break this "rule" you set for yourself, this advice encourages you to think of it as a total failure. If it cannot be redeemed and it's not acceptable, then what else could you do but throw the whole goal away?

So, maybe you say you want to go to the gym every day this month. You go for a week, then skip a few days. You say to yourself, "Well, it's all ruined now. I might as well forget about the rest of the week and start again next Monday." You discount any progress you have made, ignore the effort you have put in, and completely turn a blind eye to what caused you to skip a few days in the first place. You just throw all this away and try to get a "fresh start" at some point in the future, when you can again entertain the illusion that you are going to do things perfectly this time.

So now, instead of creating excellence, you've set up a cycle that leads only to disillusionment, wasted time, and a serious loss of confidence in yourself. Loss of confidence because any time you make a promise to yourself and fail to keep your word, you are damaging your relationship with yourself—and poor self-esteem is not far behind.

Consider replacing this kind of advice with an updated version: "Anything worth doing is worth doing poorly." This quote is from G. K. Chesterton, who wrote eighty books, two hundred short stories, and more than four thousand essays during his lifetime. His being so prolific can give us a clue to the results of *not* being perfectionists who are hellbent on all-or-nothing thinking about doing things "well."

Chesterton believed that people should in fact strive to be amateurs instead of professionals. However, in his world, the word "amateur" meant something quite different from our conventional meaning of the term (perhaps along the lines of "someone who does things kind of badly"). The word actually comes from the Latin root meaning "lover." It was first used to describe people who chose a path in life based on their love and passion for it, not the fact that it earned them money or accolades. The secret, according to Chesterton, lies in this original definition.

Of course, he wasn't saying that you shouldn't give things your best shot. He wasn't implying that you should be careless or lazy in your initial attempts, either. Rather, **it's about reframing the mindset around what we consider failure and what we consider "doing things well."** It's about taking our focus off of results and *outcomes* and being curious about what we're learning in the *process*. Of course it would be great if it were possible to start something new, become an instant expert, and impress everyone with our dazzling success on the first try. But given that this *never happens* and that thinking this way can actually make it less likely we'll succeed, it's worth adjusting our thought processes to something more realistic.

So what does it look like to "do things poorly" in the right way? What does that actually mean?

Remind Yourself that All Your Attempts Have Value

"Failure" is how you learn. It's valuable data that tells you what you need to do to be better next time. It's practice. It's an opportunity to relieve yourself of unhelpful ideas or misunderstandings. It's a chance to receive feedback.

If you remind yourself of this, then you can see that *every* attempt you make has value. Your actions don't have to result in instant success exactly as you predicted it for them to be worth something. In fact, the actions you take that go unexpectedly or force you to learn, reassess, or try harder are worth *more* than succeeding outright because they are the ones that allow you to actually grow.

When you see a successful standup comedian on stage, you only see the four or five seconds it takes them to deliver a hilarious joke and have the crowd in stitches. What you don't see is all the hours and hours of refinement that joke went through to become what it is. At that point the comedian has already delivered that same joke dozens of times to other audiences, each time with less success than what you see currently. But if the joke succeeds in its current form, it's only *because* it failed so many times before, and the comedian made notes, made improvements, and carried on. Truthfully, the comedian who has learned to do this will always outperform a new comedian who is running on raw talent alone.

If you went to the gym five times this week instead of seven, well, that's better than nothing. Bank on that. Make being bad at going to the gym the precise thing that teaches you how to be good at going to gym. Ask why you didn't go those other two times, make adjustments, and keep going. The big insight here is that your goal is not really to go to the gym seven times a week. That's just the outward results. What you really want to do is LEARN. You want to become the kind of person who always does go to the gym that often. And that learning is something you achieve with your attempts—whatever the outcome looks like.

Forget Perfection

Winston Churchill said that perfection is the enemy of progress. He was right. If you are a perfectionist or pride yourself on seeking perfection, realize right now that this is in fact a very fragile, unsustainable, and rather weak position to adopt. It is better to be creative, resilient, adaptable, forgiving, flexible, and dynamic than it is to be perfect!

Let's say you're "trying to sort your life out" and get the idea to become a minimalist and tidy up your crazy house once and for all. You have a vision in your mind: pristine, white, and perfect, with not so much as a hair out of place. You feel all zen while imagining this scene, but you open your eyes and look at what your house *really* looks like. And even though you've made good headway and done a lot to clean and declutter, all you can see is how far you are from that vision of perfection. "To hell with it" you think, and let it all run to chaos again.

The trouble was not that your house was too dirty. It was that your vision for what it could or ought to be was too perfect. If you had a little tolerance for being *in process*, you might have been able to say to yourself, "Look, obviously my house is not going to look like a museum overnight. But I've done good work tidying things up today, and that's something to be proud of." **The irony is that the person who can longest tolerate imperfection is more likely to actually achieve perfection at some point!**

Focus on Process, Not Outcome

You might announce: "I'm going to lose fifty pounds and be skinny and beautiful!"

But this goal is only the very final stage of a long, long process. It's like the last step of the marathon that takes you over the finish line—it's undoubtedly the most exciting step, but **the race itself is not achieved by that single step, but by all the thousands that came before it.** If you have your eyes fixed only on that glamorous and triumphant final step, you're ignoring the bulk of what it actually means to develop and attain something great.

In other words, all those thousands of boring steps that are taken without much fanfare, with nobody cheering you on, with no major prize or feeling of achievement—*that* is where your success actually lies. So if you desire that moment when you stand on the scale and realize you've lost fifty pounds, you need to realize that it only happens after you do the boring and difficult work of losing one pound fifty times. Ounce by ounce, choice by choice, you creep closer.

In a way, the final step is the easiest. So instead, focus on what matters, i.e., how you'll get there, not how nice it will be once you've already arrived. Say: "I'm going to walk for thirty minutes every single day," or, "I'm going to stop snacking after dinner." By making habit, behavior, and action the focus, you get to work making the outcome possible. On the other hand, if all you have to keep you motivated is the feeling of how great it'll be once you're done, you'll just fail at the first challenge. You'll lose an ounce of weight, it will be difficult and boring, you'll think you've failed, and you'll give up.

Just Start

Do you sometimes think, "Well, that's great, I'll do that . . . just as soon as winter's over/I get my promotion/we finally move home/the moon is in Sagittarius"?

It may sound strange, but sometimes procrastination and perfectionism go hand in hand. We are unwilling to start because we think we can only begin when we are perfectly ready, perfectly able, and perfectly assured that we cannot fail or flounder. But think about something that you have mastered in life—did you learn how to do it because you waited for the ideal time or had perfect support and guidance, all the resources you needed, and enough time to do what was required? Or did you just bumble along as best you could with what you had?

American author Zig Zigler said: **"You don't have to be great to start. But you have to start to be great."** It's true—beginnings can be awkward, a little embarrassing, and confusing. But every person who is an expert today began in their field with that same awkwardness and confusion. So, if there is an unavoidable stage where you must be a newbie, then why not jump in and get it over and done with as soon as possible?

The trick with this is that sometimes taking the first step is the hardest one you'll ever take. But once you do, the next step is much, much easier. And the next even easier than that. Just begin—you can think about everything else you have to do later. Just take the first step, and when that's done, you can take the next one. But in the very beginning, you don't even have to worry about the next one. Just focus on the one that's right in front of you.

Be on the lookout for procrastination that's disguised as something else. For example, you might need to make an overdue change and take a leap into the unknown . . . but you dawdle with "research" and "planning" for that next step. You tell yourself you're waiting for the right moment, but in life, nothing is ever truly risk free or perfectly easy, so you'll be waiting a long time! Put away the research, stop thinking/talking/writing about doing it, and just do it. Even if you fail outright, you're actually further along the path of progress than if you had continued to procrastinate. Even better, your action creates a certain momentum, and you've given yourself a tiny confidence boost.

Go with What Works

You told yourself you would go to the gym every day. But then you woke up one morning and felt a bit tired, and the morning after that you came down with a full-blown flu, complete with fever and rattling cough. You *can't* go to the gym now. Period.

But you can still take a gentle walk around the block. You can do some lightweight cleaning around the house and find time for some quiet yoga in your living room. Is this the same as going to the gym? Not even close. Have you reached your goal of thirty consecutive gym days? Nope. But is it the end of the world? Absolutely not.

In the real world, things happen. Our expectations go unmet, accidents happen, and things don't pan out as we wanted them to. But this isn't a problem if we have the right mindset. There is no point beating yourself up for those things that are genuinely not within your control. So, find a way to work around these limitations, adjust your plans, be flexible, and let all the rest go.

If you can't go to the gym, ask what small amount of exercise you can do—if anything. If you can't sit down for two hours and write a chapter for your book, then just try fifteen minutes and write as much as you can. If you've gone and bought a giant chocolate cake when you promised yourself you'd make better food choices, then just have one slice, not seven.

One good piece of advice is to not turn a small disaster into a big one. If you've eaten two slices of chocolate cake, okay, fine. It's done. Don't make it three! If you have the flu for a week and can't go to the gym, that's not a problem—but don't let that week turn into six months.

Chapter 2: Action Is the Beginning of Motivation

In his book *Feeling Good*, David D. Burns, MD, asks an interesting question: What comes first? Motivation or action?

Conventional wisdom tells us that we need motivation *in order to* act. After all, isn't this why motivational speakers exist? We think, perhaps unconsciously, that we need to find enough inspiration and energy before we can be roused into action. If we don't feel inspired or energetic? We usually don't act!

But Dr. Burns claims that this kind of thinking is actually backward and that it's really that **action creates motivation. Action makes you feel motivated, which in turn makes you want to do more.** Have you ever felt like you were "in the zone"? Most likely, you were enjoying the sensation of building up the momentum of motivation and inspiration.

Perhaps we can blame a self-help culture that relentlessly insists that we bring passion and drive to everything we do. We talk about dreams and desire and having enthusiasm for our life purpose. Consequently, when we inevitably feel a bit lackluster about what we're doing, we may conclude that something is wrong—maybe this *isn't* our life's calling after all, or maybe the time isn't right. Even worse, maybe it's our cue to sit back and start blaming people or situations for not somehow providing us with enough incentive.

We can make a kind of unconscious deal with ourselves that goes a little something like this: "I'll act to improve my life . . . but not yet. First I'm going to wait till it's *really* bad." The motivational speakers tell us "you've got to want it really badly!" and, because we don't really feel that, we shrug our shoulders and put off taking action till later, when maybe we'll feel more fired up.

The trouble is that the more you don't act, the easier it is to continue not acting. The opposite of momentum here is inertia—the tendency to keep on doing nothing. Whatever you were fearful about gradually starts to seem more and more scary as time goes on; whatever laziness you felt initially seems to have really cemented itself; any doubts or ambivalence seem to have embedded themselves as foregone conclusions. It's another self-fulfilling prophesy—the longer you wait to act, the harder it is to act. You might even miss opportunities or let the moment go stale as you delay and procrastinate.

The alternative is to not sit around and wait for some magical set of external conditions that finally means you are permitted to act. The alternative is not to make your action dependent on any external criteria at all—especially not some flimsy and transient feeling of "inspiration." Think of inspiration as something nice but very temporary—it's like a bright spark that gets a fire going, but it only lasts for a few seconds before disappearing.

If you want to maintain and build that fire after the spark has started it, you'll need something else: hard work.

If you're feeling uninspired, unmotivated, and lacking energy, the solution is a little counterintuitive: do something. Even if it's something small, take action. This will give you the tiniest boost of confidence and feeling of self-determination. Even small actions mean you are now *in the game*—you are no longer passive but proactively taking part in how your life unfolds. Nothing could be more encouraging than this! With this little boost in confidence, you can act again, maybe this time doing a little more.

There is no point in lamenting a lack of energy or motivation. Instead, pick a small, easy task you can do right away. Break that inertia. For example:

- You don't have the motivation to study or do schoolwork. So just commit to ten minutes and see if that boosts your interest.
- You don't feel any drive to go to the gym. That's fine. Push yourself to get up and take a walk around the block. Pay close attention to how you feel when you get back. Better? See if you actually would enjoy doing a little something more.

- You can't be bothered to reach out to your good friends and do some overdue socializing, despite knowing it's good for you. Start small and send a quick text message, just getting a conversation going. Soon, you realize it's not the huge drag you thought it would be.

As you go, you create a kind of staircase of positive feelings. Each action pulls you up out of apathy and laziness. Often, looking at a task we have to accomplish is inherently demotivating because it seems so big. But don't focus on how much you have to do—just look at the single next small step you can take right now. You'll notice that you feel a little differently once you've completed that task. The giant mountain you have to climb may seem insurmountable when you are standing far away at the very base. But if you are already on the mountain and have already taken steps on the path, the mountain doesn't seem quite so formidable as it did before.

Let's look at an example that almost everyone can identify with: cleaning the house. This is a great example because it's the kind of activity that will probably *never* create feelings of burning motivation! When was the last time you were completely jazzed up and rearing to spring clean your home?

But that doesn't mean that cleaning your home isn't a valuable, worthwhile task that you need to find time to do. Nobody really wants to do it, it's not strictly part of anyone's inspiring life vision, and it's not even really an exciting challenge. But so what? It still needs to get done.

Luckily, if you only start, you pretty quickly prove to yourself that motivation and inspiration is kind of overrated, and it's definitely not *necessary* for you to just get on and do it. Think about it: You can still clean the oven, wash the floors, and pack away your laundry in a completely foul mood. You can do the dishes despite not wanting to do the dishes. You can take out the trash while at the same time deriving no blissful sense of personal satisfaction from the task.

In a way, this is profoundly liberating. It means that *your emotional state is completely irrelevant.* Your ability to act remains as it is, regardless of how your mood or energy level changes throughout the day. You can aways act. This attitude may strike some people as a little harsh and old-fashioned, but you may find it a strange kind of relief to simply remind yourself: "I don't have to find every task pleasurable. Motivation is nice but not necessary; all that's necessary is that I act." Doesn't that make things much, much simpler?

As a side effect, taking action can create motivation. But *even if it didn't*, it's worth reminding yourself that you can always act whether you feel inspired to or not. If a task is worth doing, then do it. And that brings us to another important related concept:

Action Creates Motivation Creates Commitment

What compels you to act?

This is not an idle question but something worth thinking about carefully. Do you act simply because you feel like it? Because you *want* to act?

Inspiration and personal choice seem like natural reasons to act. After all, didn't we use our personal desire for something to help us choose a goal in the first place?

The trouble, however, is that **having a desire for an end goal is just not enough**. Merely "wanting" to act is not enough of a driver. It's a necessary condition for achievement, yes, but not a sufficient one, i.e., you certainly need it, but you also need a whole lot more if you really want to achieve the goal you've identified.

You are most likely to succeed in any endeavor if you see your action as coming from a different place entirely, that is, not just feeling like it in the moment. You need to act because you said you would. You need to act because you made a promise to yourself and possibly to others that that was what you would do. You act because you set your mind to a task and now are holding yourself to it no matter what.

The distinction between these two reasons for acting might not seem very large—until that moment when your natural inspiration and "wanting" wane. Then what?

The weakness of passion, desire, interest, motivation, and enthusiasm is that they are unreliable. They never last. They come in fits and bursts and you have very little say over how long they stick around.

On the other hand, acting because you say you will—i.e., **commitment**—is the opposite. It remains what it is regardless of where your motivation levels are. It's non-negotiable. It doesn't change with shifting energy levels or inspiration.

Commitment is the choice to act no matter what. If you are compelled to act because of a sense of commitment, then you are far, far stronger than if you are powered by the insubstantial and limited fuel of motivation/inspiration.

Taking action creates motivation, but it also reinforces a sense of commitment. Imagine this: If you are already in a twenty-year-long marriage, that momentum, that "winning streak," is far harder to jeopardize than a superficial two-week love affair. In other words, the more committed you are, the easier it is to remain committed. The more action you create, the more motivation you drum up to act again. In time, this repeated action builds confidence because you are in effect keeping your own promises to yourself. This builds self-trust and self-respect.

What does a committed mindset actually look like, though?

Many of us falsely believe that we are committed to our goals, when really the only things holding us to certain actions are the temporary feeling of wanting to and the transitory sensations of reward when we do act. But commitment goes further than this—it is the ability act with dedication, devotion, and responsibility, *independent of how easy or pleasurable that action might be*.

To see if you're truly committed to your goals, simply look at how much airtime you're currently giving to various excuses and justifications. Let's say you've decided on the goal to lose weight and get in better shape. Look closely at any of these "reasons" you can't act, and you will see just how firm your resolve and commitment really is.

For example, you set the goal of losing a few pounds and giving up on the bad habit of eating cheap processed chocolate every day. Your initial enthusiasm is okay for a few days, and you successfully avoid the temptation to munch on candy bars. But then after around a week or so, your resolve flags a little and you cave in and binge on a small mountain of chocolate. You explain this behavior to yourself like this:

"It's not such a big deal. I've been really good for ages. I deserve a little treat."
"I wouldn't want to become one of those boring, militant people who go on and on about healthy eating. I mean, what if I give myself an eating disorder!?"
"But they were on a two-for-one special. I couldn't pass up such a good deal."
"Chocolate isn't *really* that bad for you; it's a bit of a myth. After all, cocoa contains plant phenols and, uh, this *Snickers* bar is rich in peanuts . . . so it's actually a high protein snack."

When you notice yourself coming up with "reasons" like this, try to replace them in your mind with what you are actually saying: "My promises to myself are not worth keeping, and my word means nothing." The "reasons" are just a million different red herrings—they are nothing more than a distraction.

This may seem harsh, but it may reframe your choices and remind you of what is genuinely at stake when you fail to follow through on commitments you assign yourself. To return to the marriage example—nobody makes marriage vows that say, "I promise to be faithful and loving to you . . . until I don't feel like it anymore." Present divorce statistics notwithstanding, the *whole point* of a marriage vow is that you mean it. You keep your vow because you made it. You don't keep it because you weren't sufficiently tempted to break it. You don't keep it because it's easy and convenient in the moment to do so. You keep it because that is what you determined to do.

Making a marriage vow with caveats is no different from saying, "I promise to myself not to eat cheap nasty chocolate every day . . . until I don't feel like it anymore." Commitment is about detaching your action from any external, fleeting conditions and making it a **promise**. Imagine this promise is so rock-solid, so firm and unmovable, that you never even consider not following through with it. That's how solid your resolve needs to be if it hopes to withstand everything that would threaten to erode it.

You might ride the wave of initial enthusiasm for a while, and you might succeed in avoiding chocolate simply because none was offered to you and you weren't exposed to it. You might keep your "promise" very well ... while it's convenient. But avoiding chocolate is a bit like marriage—it's not always easy. You need to make goals and commit yourself to them "in sickness and in health, for richer and poorer." In other words, you need to adopt the mindset that whatever happens in life is simply irrelevant and has zero impact on how you ultimately act. So you hear all the very many excuses and justifications, and you think to yourself, "So what?"

"But I'm exhausted."
"So what?"
"I'm not even sure if I still want to do this."
"So what?"
"It's expensive."
"So what?"
"I don't actually have the time."
"So what?"

Your mind will come up with endless reasons not to. But when you are committed, none of it matters. Look at every single objection your mind comes up with and shrug your shoulders. It has no bearing on anything.

Act as you said you would. *Because* you said you would.

Summary:

- There is one key feature that separates those strategies that work from those that never do: action. At some point, if you truly wish to transform your life, you will need to cross over from where you are to where you want to be—by taking action.
- To craft an action for bias, drop the belief that you need to be excellent at something the first time around, and replace it with: "Anything worth doing is worth doing poorly." Strive to be an amateur and not a professional.
- Remind yourself that all your attempts have value and that failure is valuable because it's how you learn. Abandon the need to be perfect and focus on the process of learning and growing, rather than any flashy outcome. Learn to tolerate the imperfection of being a beginner.

- Just start—"You don't have to be great to start. But you have to start to be great." Every expert began as a newbie, so just take the first step and trust that it gets easier. Go with what works and don't allow a minor disaster to turn into a major one.
- Conventional wisdom tells us that we need motivation in order to act, but it's really the other way around: action creates motivation. Taking action breaks inertia and builds confidence and momentum—and you don't *need* to be inspired to take the first step.
- Don't wait for a perfect set of external conditions to give you permission to act. If you're feeling uninspired and unmotivated and lacking energy, the solution is a little counterintuitive: do something, even if it's small. Act from commitment, not from temporary inspiration.

Part 2: What Does Success Really Take?

Chapter 3: Get Comfortable with Risk

Perhaps when you hear the word "risk-taker," you think of something akin to "thrill-seeker," i.e., someone who enjoys flinging themselves out of airplanes or handling venomous snakes for fun. If you're someone who doesn't think of themselves this way, you might believe that *not* looking for this kind of trouble is the smarter way to live. Perhaps you imagine the best strategy is staying put, keeping the status quo and not rocking the boat.

According to Bill Aulet, a senior lecturer at the Massachusetts Institute of Technology Sloan School of Management, this is actually an illusion. He says in many cases **doing things the way they've always been done** is the "**most risky thing you can probably do**"—especially in business. Choosing to forfeit your choice is a choice, and a lack of action is, in its own way, an action—it's the action of keeping us right where we are. When you don't take a risk to change something in your life, you are in effect saying that you are happy with the status quo and *are choosing it.*

Importantly, this is NOT the same as taking a blind gamble and leaping into something without a clear strategy. Instead, we might allow our fear and doubt to get the better of us, and tell ourselves a story that makes *any* risk seem scary and foolish. We might start to place reasonable risk in the "thrill-seeker" category or assume that anything attempted with less than one hundred percent certainty of success is foolish. This may sound like prudence and wisdom talking, but it's really nothing more than fear.

Behind an inability to take action may be plain old fear. Someone tells us "there's a chance this might not work," and we hear "it won't work . . . so don't bother." Throwing yourself mindlessly into risky endeavors is as bad as never taking any risk at all—and that's because both come at a cost. Inside your comfort zone, things are safe and predictable, but they're also potentially stale and small. Outside your comfort zone is a world of potential growth, novelty, and achievement, but it's also a place of potential loss, humiliation, or danger.

This leaves us in a curious predicament. If we want to stay safe, we forfeit growth and novelty. And if we want to grow and experience that novelty, we have to forfeit our safety. **There is no way in life to have both safety and growth!**

But it's always your choice. When you make this choice, bear in mind, however, that you may still experience setbacks, disappointment, pain, and humiliation even if you stay in your comfort zone. And remember, too, that even if you step out of your comfort zone and the worst happens, there is still inevitably some value in taking a chance, challenging yourself, and learning something new in the process.

Risk-averse people have made an assessment, or a risk-benefit analysis. It's one that seems justified on the surface, but the more you look at it, the less sense it really makes. To prove this to yourself, all you need to do is find someone in their old age who consistently chose never to take risks, try something new, challenge themselves, or be uncomfortable. Find a person who never put themselves out there, never tried something different, never took a leap of faith. What kind of life do they lead? Is it one filled with integrity, pride, confidence, satisfaction, grit, curiosity, and the hunger to keep growing? Chances are, it's none of these things. It's only one thing—comfortable. If you remain in your comfort zone for all your life, that's precisely what you'll be. But that's *all* you'll be.

If, however, you take (calculated!) risks, then your life may well be filled with some additional disappointments, adversities, challenges, and losses compared to if you had stayed put. But it will also be filled with commensurate feelings of self-worth, knowledge, understanding, resilience, accomplishment, and hope.

It's Normal to Feel Fear

Despite what some self-styled entrepreneurs on LinkedIn would have you believe, success in life is not about feeling invulnerable. It's not about having eternal rock-solid confidence that never wavers, a can-do positive attitude, and the go-getter mindset that makes you wake up at 4 a.m. every morning to say affirmations and feel invincible.

But the truth is that it's not necessary to feel invincible. Fear is a normal and predictable experience. **Our goal should never be to be without fear, but rather to change our attitude toward it**. One way of putting it is that fear is always allowed to be a passenger in the car of your life, but it should never be allowed to be the driver!

We all vary somewhat in the degree to which we can tolerate uncertainty, the unknown, and the risks associated with it. Your personality, your age, whether you're male or female, and the culture you grew up in all influence how you perceive risk and what you consider a tolerable threshold. Men, for example, possess more testosterone, which has been shown to correlate with risk-taking behavior and may allow men to act on impulse far more often than women do (for better and for worse!). On the other hand, you may simply have learned certain behaviors toward risk or may be in a stage of life that heavily favors inaction over action (for example, you're older, you're a new parent, or you feel like your mental or physical resources are too low to take on too much risk).

Whatever your current state, though, ask yourself this question:

Am I completely, one hundred percent happy with my life as it is right now and don't want anything to change?

If the answer to the above is "no," then that's a sign that you will need to come out of your comfort zone sooner or later. And that means that you will need to court some level of risk. The fact is that if we want to take any degree of control over our lives to grow and evolve, to learn something, or to strive for something better, then risk is involved. The inverse of the above question is the understanding that if you don't take any risk at all, ever, then your life will stay exactly as it is now (or, who knows, maybe it will passively get worse).

It is a mistake to think that fear of the unknown is some kind of problem. Sometimes we are faced with a big change, a choice, or a challenge, and we feel fear. We interpret this fear to mean that we are doing something wrong. Maybe *we* are wrong and need to turn back and head into the comfort zone as soon as possible, right? We think that being uncomfortable, uncertain, or a little afraid is a sign that we are doing things poorly. Maybe we imagine that all those successful people we see in the news embark on their life projects with ease and confidence. We imagine that all the ultra-accomplished people started out already somehow knowing that it would all work out for them.

But they didn't! They were scared, just like you. They did not know how it would pan out, just like you. The first big mindset shift, then, is to understand that arrogance, bravado, and invulnerability are all a lie—nobody feels like that, and you are not *required* to feel like that to succeed. The corollary is that feeling terrified is not proof that something is wrong or that you should stop what you're doing. **You are not required to be fearless, but courageous**. Taking a strategic risk can still *feel* super scary. But what makes a risk calculated and intelligent is that you don't allow this knee-jerk fear to control you or make decisions for you. That's where courage comes in.

How to Take Smart Risks

Fear is built into the way you appraise things. When encountering the unknown or something new, your brain will tend to conjure up images and ideas of everything that could go wrong or memories of when it did go wrong in the past. It feels bad and it's self-limiting . . . but it also keeps you safe. It's a big part of why your ancestors survived, and we can thank this part of the mind for helping us learn and adapt. But while you can acknowledge the fear's presence and thank it for bringing your attention to potential dangers, you can also consciously invite your higher brain to weigh in, too.

Step 1: Identify something you want

What are your deepest desires? This goes beyond simply noticing what could be better about the status quo. What are your dreams? What is something you have yet to achieve or learn that would add enormous richness and meaning to your life? Take some time to understand what these things are, and you tap into a power source.

Step 2: Assess the possible risks to getting it

Once you've identified your life's grander dreams and desires, then weigh up the risks. But don't just tally up the costs of taking action toward that dream. Tally up the costs of not acting, and offset them against both the benefits of staying the same and the benefits of reaching your goal. In other words:

The cost of acting

The cost of not acting

The benefit of acting

The benefit of not acting

Smart risk means appraising all of these—not just one or two. Spend some time examining the form any potential risks could take. Just because you're risk averse, it doesn't mean you're good at processing risk. After all, you may be so terrified of something that you have no real idea about what it actually is. So actually pause and understand what you're dealing with, its size and shape, and the likelihood of various outcomes. Give things a name.

Step 3: Think about the impact of those risks

Understanding a risk and understanding the *impact* of that risk on your life are two different things. For example, if you're thinking about starting your own business, you may be worried about the possibility of taking longer to launch than anticipated. Now, this may be a very real outcome, and it could indeed take months and months before your new business starts showing any promise. But what would be the impact of this worst-case scenario on your life? Perhaps you have ample savings, a partner to support you, or a reliable part-time job to keep you going. In this case, taking a longer time to get off the ground won't have that big of an impact on you—even if it feels terrifying to think about. Or maybe you consider the risks and realize that certain dangers are bigger than you first thought.

On the other hand, you may consider starting your own business risky, but the impact of succeeding in it would be such a positive force in your life it may turn out to be the single best thing you've ever accomplished. Similarly, it may be the case that as great as a positive outcome would be, it doesn't necessarily follow that everything in your life would be permanently improved. Until you really stop to consider how it would feel to either fail or succeed, you won't really know how to rank risks and make smart choices. Take another look at the risks and benefits from the previous step and assign a numerical figure to each so you can properly compare them against one another.

Step 4: Assign each risk a probability

What's the *likelihood* of each risk or benefit actually coming to be? Be as accurate and honest as you can, and leave something blank if you genuinely don't know the answer. Use a scale from one to five, with five having the greatest chance of happening and one having the lowest chance, for example. This helps you keep perspective.

When you're doing a risk assessment, you are looking at the combination of the impact of a hazard, as well as the likelihood of it actually happening. For example, you may be diagnosed with an illness and offered a drug that occasionally kills the people who take it. The negative consequences are extreme (death!), but you may go for the drug anyway because the likelihood of that outcome is very, very small (let's say it's something like a one in ten million chance).

To your mind, *every* potential danger is real and serious. Your brain evolved to err on the side of false positives (you don't act when you should) instead of false negatives (you didn't act when you should have) because the second type of error can kill you, whereas the worst that can happen with the first is some mild regret or a lost opportunity.

It works when thinking of benefits, too. Many people continue to play the lottery despite vanishingly small chances of winning because if they *did* win, the sheer size of the positives would be lifechanging. Likewise it's easier to put up with a negative outcome that might happen (maybe a likelihood of one or two) if it leads to a more likely positive outcome (let's say a likelihood of five).

Step 5: Make a plan

Too many people start their "risk assessment" here and leap into plan-making before they've properly considered what the options are. But do this only as the *final* step, and allow your actions to be guided by the numbers you've assigned to each risk and benefit. Ask yourself:

What risk is it possible to eliminate or mitigate?
Which risks might be worth taking given their potential benefits?
What is the cost of the status quo?
Are there some positives to the worst-case scenario?
Will taking an action, any action, improve your position, regardless of the outcome?
How would someone with your values choose to act in this scenario?
What's the worst that could happen?
What's the BEST that could happen?

Some people are born to take risks. They question the way things are, face problems head-on, and look for new ways to do things. Those who aren't born to take risks are a little more "security oriented." They don't dislike or even admire people who take risks. It's just that they like stability and comfort. When it comes to some things, it's nice to feel like you're in charge.

Both types of people bring value to the world. People who take risks change the world, while people who don't take risks keep the world safe. But just as risk-takers need limits (they shouldn't take all the risks they face all the time), people who *don't* like to take risks need to be willing to push themselves from time to time. Both categories need a systematic strategy that offsets the worst of their tendencies.

Chapter 4: Understanding the Four Levels of Action

Grant Cardone is an author, sales trainer, and speaker, as well as the original proponent of the idea of "four levels of action." According to him, action is not just a binary—i.e., doing it or not doing it—but something that falls into four distinct categories:

1. Doing nothing

2. Retreating

3. Normal levels of action

4. Massive action

For Cordone, **nothing worthwhile in life happens by accident, but by you taking**

action. The greater the action you take, the bigger the chances of success. If you can take the right level of action and be disciplined, persistent, and consistent in that action, then you will succeed. In fact, according to Cordone, doing so is more likely to predict your success than any other factor.

Let's start with the first one—doing nothing. It's what it sounds like. You are not doing anything in life to change anything, learn something new, acquire something, move forward, gain control or mastery, or create. You are staying still. Retreating is actually taking action but with results in the reverse direction. Instead of making a change, you dig deeper into the status quo and act to undo any gains or cancel out any advances. It sounds counterintuitive, but this sort of action is often attempted because of imagined negative outcomes of taking action.

Normal levels of action are also what they sound like. This is the realm where behaving achieves you a kind of **average** outcome. Normal lives, marriages, careers, and lifestyles that are considered conventional and sufficient. This compares drastically with massive action, which Cordone views as an entirely new level of operation. In fact, he sees action taken at this level as actually creating new problems with unreasonable actions—that then warrant further unreasonable actions.

At the same time, the realm of massive action is the place where real transformation, big success, and evolution occur. The difference between normal action and massive action is, according to Cordone, the big difference between an unremarkable person and one who has made a real success of their lives. The trick is that most of us think that normal levels of action are . . . well, normal. We think it's enough to do just enough, and then achieve a kind of middling averageness. Cordone is super clear on this: Normal action will never get supernatural results. He asks people to really think about what "average" is and if they really want that for themselves. The average person reads around one book a year, works only as much as they need to, is risk averse, avoids challenge, and earns and achieves at a totally predictable and unremarkable level.

Then, **when normal action encounters resistance, obstacles, competition,**

adversity, or self-doubt, what happens? It is knocked back down and becomes worth even less than average. Giving any area of your life only middling amounts of attention and effort can never be a winning strategy because eventually that effort will dwindle and subside, producing very little. Massive action is, in fact, required to blast through obstacles, make genuine transformations, and achieve worthy goals.

In other words, our biggest problem when it comes to taking action may be that we simply underestimate just how much action is required. We may embark on grand plans, expecting that a normal level of effort and input will be enough. It's not simply that our actions are insufficient, but that our entire mindset is characterized by a set of beliefs about what is required of us. So, imagine that someone is intelligent, positive, and motivated, but they have the idea that they can beat out ninety percent of their competitors without breaking a sweat. This may be an unconscious and not fully realized idea, but it's there nonetheless, quietly ensuring mediocre outcomes at best.

The mindset comes along with other self-sabotaging sentiments such as:

- If I'm truly "meant to" do something or have something, it will be easy and the path obvious
- I should strive for balance in life and *always* give equal time to rest and recreation
- I can wait for someone to offer me an opportunity, for permission, or for the right time to start
- I am a good person, so in a sense I deserve good things and can expect them
- Steady, consistent habit is what counts—so I only have to focus on these little steps
- I should never have to feel humiliated, confused, exhausted, afraid, or disappointed
- Adversity isn't fair or right, so therefore I don't have to do anything to prepare for it
- If I do the right thing, that matters. Quality over quantity. Intention is what counts
- Incremental changes can lead to drastic evolution; incremental changes can lead to exponential growth

If we're honest, most of us subscribe to some extent to the above ideas, even if not consciously. Perhaps we have been lied to and told that success is for those who are just effortlessly genius or lucky or who find a way to casually create an exceptional life without *doing* anything exceptional. But all of that is an illusion. Nobody falls into an outstanding success without action and effort of a corresponding magnitude.

Let's again imagine the task of becoming an author. This requires not just crafting a complete and high-quality original work, but also making sure that you are promoting that work to people who have the ability to have it published and widely read, or else learning how to self-publish and market the book yourself. Becoming a successful author from scratch takes *phenomenal levels of effort*. It's really, really hard work!

But let's say you buy into some of the mindset described above, and you have a deep belief in yourself as a natural author with real talent. Let's say that for five whole years, you tell people that you're an author, when in fact you have never actually completed a single manuscript, and you have no regular writing routine, have completed no courses, belong to no writing groups, and have no current plans for a story of any kind. You're at level one—you're doing nothing, and your results will be nothing. Yes, it's true that some authors succeed by luck or having access to connections and resources you don't. But even they could not achieve a thing unless they made *some* effort, right?

Let's say you eventually realize that you are going to have to work, though. You have a wild dream: you picture seeing your book in all the big bookstores, you see your face in the newspapers, and you watch your bank account swell as the profits come in from your international best-seller. And what's that, do you see a Nobel Prize for literature on the horizon? Great! Dreaming big is a beautiful thing. But let's imagine that in order to achieve this massive dream, you decide to sit in a café for an hour every Sunday morning and "work on" your novel (i.e., scratch out around one or two thousand words). Well, except if it's rainy. Or if you're on vacation. Sometimes it's only a few hundred words. Can you see how the goal and the effort level do not even remotely belong in the same universe?

Imagine that you have identified a goal of wanting to lose forty pounds. You decide to switch from white rice to brown rice, and put skim milk in your coffee instead of full fat. At the end of a month, you actually weigh more than when you started because you also had three "self-care" cheat days where you took a break from your grueling diet to eat cake and pizza. Again, the effort and the size of the goal are not aligned.

If these examples seem too obvious to you, ask yourself honestly if you are not currently expecting dramatic results in some area of your life without making any dramatic efforts. Of course, there is nothing really wrong with being mediocre. If you have a goal you're passionate about (getting your MBA, raising happy kids, building a boat), you might make that your priority and consciously decide that other areas in your life can be mediocre. So you prioritize your career and put your fitness on the back burner, focus on your kids and downplay the value of creative expression, or dedicate every hour to building that boat, knowing you can tidy your house some other time. That's fine. The problem arises when you know that something is a passion and a priority for you and expect that mediocre input will somehow translate to meteoric success.

Cordone is big on **duty, obligation, and responsibility**. This means being a grownup about your goals and realizing that YOU are in charge of achieving them. If you forfeit that responsibility, the best you can ever expect is to be kind of middling. If you don't take ownership of your mistakes, you can't do anything to correct them.

What Massive Action Looks Like

Massive action means consistently doing more than the average person under similar conditions. It means going beyond what is expected as "normal." It also means acting according to one's purpose, drive, desire, and life vision.

It's easy to "think big," but the real challenge comes in follow-through. To be truly impactful, "massive" action can sometimes just mean incredibly focused, targeted action. If we have worked out what matters and what gets results and apply ourselves relentlessly to doing only those things, this is massive action. By the same token, we can do big, flashy actions that are useless since they lack any real strategy. So, don't get too hung up on "massive" meaning highly visible, risky, dramatic, or arrogant!

Step 1: What is your goal?

You can't take massive action if you're not even really clear about what you want. Wishy-washy goals always fail—think about it, how could they be achieved when they don't strictly exist? Your goal needs to be concrete and realistic.

What do you want?
What specifically do you want?
What will that look and feel like?
What are all the steps from where you are to this end point?
How will you know when the goal is achieved?
Is there a deadline?
Where and when are you going to take action toward it (implementation intention)?

Step 2: Resign yourself to the fact of hard work

Truthfully, many people conjure up a great-sounding goal and then . . . do nothing. Being clear about your desires is great, but it doesn't guarantee you a thing. People can hold themselves back simply because they have not psychologically made the leap into hard work. They sense that embarking for real on the goal would mean leaving behind a certain ease and comfort, and they would prefer to not struggle or feel awkward, uncertain, or tired. So they stay in their comfort zone, never really starting. We've explored these ideas already—procrastination, perfectionism—all these things are simply an unwillingness to embrace the discomfort that change always brings. And that includes good change that we say we want!

You cannot take massive action half-heartedly or by accident. You are required to face your fear head-on and engage with the idea of rejection, criticism, mistakes, and the blood, sweat, and tears of hard work that may nevertheless result in failure. For some people, it's preferable to hold on to unfulfilled potential than to actually try to find out for sure that they do not have what it takes. So, it's easier to say "I could have been a brilliant author" than it is to roll up your sleeves and *do* it and face up to how good an author you really are.

Step 2 may be the most difficult of all since it requires an almost supernatural level of courage. We need to be honest with ourselves about the hard work that is in store for us if we mean it when we say we want to achieve our dreams. There are no guarantees. And while it's possible to distract yourself with superficial busy work, deep down you know that this doesn't really move you forward. The only forward is through discomfort—there is no cheat code, no shortcut, and no special hack that gets you around the discomfort. Make peace with that!

Step 3: Commit yourself

Action is great. But you cannot act just once. You need to act that way again and again and again. Think of it like marriage. You make your vows once, but really, your commitment comes in every single choice you make every day after that vow. You need to be unwavering.

It helps to literally write down your commitment to yourself. Create a "contract" where you outline exactly what promises you are making to yourself—what you will do, when, and how. Don't think in terms of grand single gestures, but in terms of consistent habit. What will you do *every day*? Write down your rituals and routines. Increase your chances of following your contract by making a public declaration or asking an accountability partner to hold you to your word.

Step 4: Know the price of success and pay it willingly

Every goal costs something. Every success that is worth anything WILL take its toll on you. So what is the cost, and how will you bear it?

You might need to sacrifice time, energy, and resources. You might need to let go of something else that is also important to you. You might need to pass up on pleasurable activities or forego certain treats and comforts. Going even deeper, your entire life might change—*you* might change. The way you think about life and yourself may be permanently altered; you may take on a heightened sense of responsibility for the rest of your life. Take on these costs with open eyes. Just because you are pursuing your life's dream, it doesn't mean that everything will be perfect and painless once you've achieved it!

Step 6: Light a fire under your butt

Finally, you'll need a sense of urgency. Writing a novel, for example, takes time—lots of it. Start now! Don't assume that you have all the time in the world. It's later than you think. Saying "one day" is the same as saying "never." Don't forget that part of your journey will be missteps, accidents, and failures. These take time, too.

You are not rushing, but at the same time nobody ever relaxed their way into incredible success. Be brisk, energetic, and driven. Set deadlines and *go for it*—not tomorrow, but now. Your goal should be of such all-engrossing energy in your mind that it keeps you up at night and pops into your head first thing in the morning. It has to be something you can't pull yourself away from. Dig deep and find that energy source that will fire you up—whether that's a sense of purpose, a duty to others, a life vision, or even just the vanity of proving everyone wrong.

Be a little "unreasonable" in your actions. Be a little excessive and allow yourself to become obsessed by your goal. The alternative is usually mediocrity.

Chapter 5: How to Overcome Resistance: Externalize It

According to author Steven Pressfield, there is one main reason that people fail to take action when they really want to: **resistance**.

Internal fears, procrastination, self-sabotage, avoidance, and self-doubt are all forms of resistance that can prevent you from taking action—especially, in the case of Pressfield's work, *creative action*. In his renowned book *The War of Art*, Pressfield explores the idea of resistance and gives readers advice on how to push past it.

Let's say that you're trying to complete a project that requires an enormous amount of creative input—for example, writing a novel. You have always wanted to write one and know that you would derive enormous satisfaction from the challenge and from seeing the completed work transformed from abstract ideas in your head into something real on the page. And yet, as compelled as you are to achieve all this, you sit down day after day in front of the blank page and produce *nothing.*

Is it writer's block? Are you simply a poor writer? Pressfield would say that all you are experiencing is garden variety resistance—that nagging inner voice that questions you, puts you down, and tells you that your efforts will be for nothing so you might as well give up. This internal and self-defeating force seems trivial, but it is powerful enough to consistently stand between you and the things you know you want.

Pressfield talks about this force like he would a force of nature—something constantly pushing against your efforts. **It's all the negative thought patterns, blind spots, low self-esteem, self-biases, laziness, and plain old fear that keep us unable to act**. Even worse, the more we procrastinate or avoid our task, the more our inner resistance might encourage us to think of this delay itself as proof that we are incompetent. It's not just artists who struggle with this—any time you are trying to create something new, you may encounter resistance, whether you're trying to invent something, compose clear communication, or launch a business endeavor.

Pressfield states it clearly: "You are not your resistance." He makes this point again and again to emphasize the fact that procrastinating on a task is **not** proof that you should give up, or evidence of your lack of ability or competence. Simply, feeling resistance is normal and not a reason to give in or give up. All it really is? A common reluctance that all human beings experience during the creative process, and nothing to get worked up about. The only response we can have is to acknowledge it and take action anyway.

So, if you sit down and find yourself unable to write a single sentence, your mind might start up with a complicated internal stream of self-doubt and criticism:

This is hopeless, and your idea is really boring, anyway. Why don't you wait till you have something interesting to say?

Admit it, you have zero skill as an author.

Oh my God, even if you did finish this stupid book, can you imagine how embarrassing it's going to be when everyone reads it?

Okay—so you're encountering resistance. But what do you do once you realize this? Let's say you start psychoanalyzing yourself and trying to argue back to the inner critic:

Maybe you're this way because your parents always told you that artists are selfish and deluded. Maybe that's why.

You ARE a talented author. You just need to believe in yourself. Maybe do some affirmations or something.

Maybe it's because you never went to a university, and you've got something to prove. Why have you always felt that others look down on you for that?

But guess what? All of the above is *still* resistance. Talking about resistance is resistance. Feeling bad about having resistance—also resistance. **You might be wondering what *isn't* resistance. That's easy: taking action.** Wanting to figure out all the ins and outs of the emotional reasons why you're not taking action is just a trap in the disguise of a solution—if it isn't action, it isn't moving you forward. If you fret over why you're not taking action and get embroiled in complex explanations, justifications, and interpretations, recognize that this is just another form your resistance is taking. The longer you engage, the longer you delay in doing what actually matters—the work itself.

Pressfield claims, then, that "you are not the problems that stand in your way. The problems are the problems. Work the problems." That's all. Time spent on introspection, questioning, self-criticism, and so on is just time that could be better spent getting on with the work at hand.

Two Ways to Overcome Resistance

Pressfield says there are two main approaches you can take. You can wage war against your resistance, or you can "befriend the dragon." Both techniques require that you externalize this resistance as something that is not a part of you or your process—and so it can be handled at a psychological distance.

Option 1: Wage War

Imagine, says Pressfield, that your resistance is a formidable dragon, and you the artist are a brave knight who has to vanquish the beast. You must fight it, and you must win. It may help to think of resistance as an enemy to vanquish because it can activate feelings of competition and opposition. Framing your mission in terms of myth this way triggers a deep psychological sense that you are not alone—after all, the knight is equipped with a sword and armor, maybe a trusty steed, and a powerful sense that good always triumphs over evil in the end.

This is another psychological benefit—the feeling that you are, ultimately, "good" and that you are valiantly questing against something that is unnatural and not at all a part of you. This framework provides a strong sense of energy, purpose, and power and can speak to a part of yourself that wants justice and goodness and wants to be strong and courageous in the face of something that would threaten everything you hold dear.

It's worth mentioning that Pressfield is an ex-marine, so you can understand why personal mythology like this would appeal so much to him. In his book *Do the Work*, he writes "Resistance is an active, intelligent, protean, malign force—tireless, relentless, and inextinguishable—whose sole object is to stop us from becoming our best selves and from achieving our higher goals." Here are the steps he recommends for battling that "malign force":

Step 1: Give the dragon a name

This externalizes it and gives the concept a psychological "handle." Make this name a shorthand for all the reasons behind the resistance—you're not going to dwell on these reasons or rehash them again and again. You're just going to slap a label on the whole mess and move on. Let's say you call your resistance "Fatso" or "Who Cares" to emphasize the lack of bother you're going to show it.

Step 2: Ignore the dragon

One trick the dragon can pull is to lure you into completely unnecessary battle in the first place. You could sit down to write, gird your loins, and prepare yourself for a massive face-off . . . but why do that when you can just quickly get started before your resistance even has time to wake up and start challenging you to a fight. You don't have to be ready or have an argument or a big analytical session before you can start. Just start.

Step 3: Fight the dragon

Sure, once you just start, you might find Who Cares bursting onto the scene with extra force. Fine. The dragon wants to stop you by any means necessary. The way you win against the dragon is to not stop. This bit's important: If you turn away from your work and focus instead of stabbing at the dragon, you've already lost, since the dragon has succeeded in getting your attention off what matters. No, your task is to blast through the dragon's distractions and continue on your path, undeterred no matter what. Move faster than the dragon. Don't get lured in or trapped.

Step 4: Take a break

Pressfield says, "Some days you win and some days you lose. *Why* you lost doesn't matter. It only matters that you start again." That said, you can take a break to recharge, regroup, and build your energy up. This is **not** the same as avoidance or procrastination. Instead, it's about temporarily relieving the pressure so you can recuperate. Go for a long walk, give your brain some breathing room, think of something else for a moment, and return to your task later, feeling refreshed.

The truth is that warring with the dragon takes energy. The dragon is enormous, strong, and persistent. It has far, far more energy than you do and is hellbent on standing in your way. Plus, a dragon never really dies—luckily, though, you don't have to kill it. You just need to consistently keep it away long enough to get your work done. Knowing that the dragon is always ready to rear its ugly head later on actually empowers you. That's because you're not surprised or dismayed when it happens—you're expecting it and already know what your response will be: carry on doing the work anyway, just like always.

So, you sit down to do some writing, but find yourself browsing nonsense online for a half hour before you realize what you're doing. You become aware that you've gotten distracted, and feel a pang of shame, self-doubt, and all the rest flood into you. "Oh, hello, Who Cares! I see it's you again." It takes enormous presence of mind and strength, but you look at all the feelings of guilt, doubt, and shame and shrug your shoulders, turning away from them. Instead of going down some mental rabbit hole where you have an inner debate about screen addiction or ruminate over whether you should self-diagnose with "demand avoidance," you put on your work hat and take action. At first it's literally one sentence on a page, and it's not genius. But then you take a deep breath and write another.

"But there are people out there who are real authors, you know, and what you're doing looks nothing like that . . ." You hear this inner voice and ignore it. You don't argue with it. You just take a deep breath and put down a third sentence. This is what a daily battle against the dragon feels like.

Option 2: Befriend the Dragon

Granted, you might not be an ex-marine like Pressfield and find the war metaphor less compelling. For some of us, labeling something an enemy and using imagery of violence and force against it actually makes us fear that thing more. We activate our stress response and make our experience A Big Problem when it really isn't. Plus, we may have a nagging suspicion that our resistance wasn't some senseless beast, but a force that is at least in some part there to help us, protect us, or share an important message.

If this sounds like you, then it may be worth your while to befriend the dragon, rather than wanting to chop its head off. This takes the attitude that you and your resistance just have different opinions, but that this doesn't mean you have to go to war about it.

Step 1: Say thank you

Okay, so your resistance has made an appearance. Be grateful! Imagine that your resistance is actually trying to guide and protect you. It's not a nasty adversary but a force that's deserving of our respect, attention, empathy, and understanding. Note, however, that this doesn't mean agreement and immediate acquiescence—only that you will engage politely and give the resistance the civility it deserves.

Step 2: Actually listen

What is your resistance trying to tell you? This means not judging yourself for having resistance, and not judging the resistance for existing at all. In fact, be curious about any judgment that comes up—where did it really come from? What purpose does it think it's serving? You may discover these knee-jerk reactions come from past memories or old triggers.

Step 3: Ask the dragon useful questions

The dragon might have an important message or a much-needed lesson to teach you. The trouble with dragons is that they often want to talk about quite difficult, sometimes painful things, so we need to be very willing to listen and be honest about what we hear. This is not the same as agreeing with the dragon when it tells you that you're a loser and everything you do will fail. Rather, it's about understanding the nature of your more deep-seated concerns. Ask:

What are you actually resisting?
What is the dragon protecting you from?

What does the dragon think will happen if you carry on down the path to the goal? What is the dragon afraid will happen?

One good technique is to ask three questions in a row to get to the root of the resistance. For example:

"Okay, Who Cares, what are you so afraid will happen, anyway?"
"I'm afraid that everyone will read this book when you're done!"
"And so? What would that mean if everyone did read it?"
"It would mean that we'd be exposed and everyone would know what we're really like."
"And so what would that mean? If everyone knew what we were really like?"
"It would mean that they could reject us. We might lose friends or be abandoned."

So there is the root of the resistance: You cannot finish your book because if you do, it might mean you lose all your friends and are rejected and abandoned. So, the dragon is not a mindless menace getting in the way, but is just scared and trying to protect you from pain and trouble.

Step 4: Be discerning

Now you have to be very careful. We've already seen that it can be a trap to get too tangled up with endless engagement with the dragon. So you have to consciously sort out the difference between

- Irrational dragon worries
- Realistic concerns

Though your dragon can call your attention to something worth noting, it doesn't mean that it's wise—the wisdom comes from what you choose to do with certain negative thoughts and fears. When you are discerning, you hear the dragon's warning ("people are going to reject you") and you pay attention, but you don't take it at face value. You ask:

Do I have evidence to believe this?
What can I do practically to prevent this from happening?
Is this really the big scary thing I think it is?
Can I moderate this sentiment so it's more accurate?
So, when the dragon chips in with its fears and warnings, you are better equipped to *respond* to it by saying something like, "Sure,

it's likely that not everyone will like my work, but that's not the end of the world, and even if people don't like my novel, that doesn't mean they will completely reject me as a person. Every author has their critics—that's normal and far from the end of the world."

Step 5: Keep taking action

Then you just get to work. The dragon will chip in again, and you'll say thank you, perhaps noting down its concerns and politely telling it you will take a look later—once you've done your tasks for the day. Maybe the dragon flags a genuine weakness or blind spot for your attention, and that's great. But your main task in befriending the dragon is to dispense with their concerns in the most rational way and get back to work as quickly as possible.

Summary:

- Choosing the status quo (foregoing action) is still a choice, and it comes with risks—sometimes it's the riskiest choice. There is no way to remain in your comfort zone and grow at the same time, so learn to take

strategic, conscious, and deliberate risks with the understanding that it's normal to feel fear. Fear is normal but doesn't have to be in the driver's seat.
- Be courageous not fearless; identify your goal and appraise the risks to going for it, the impact the goal will have on you, and the cost of not taking the risk. Then make a rational plan for how to mitigate those risks according to their probability of happening.
- According to Grant Cordone, there are four main levels of action: doing nothing, retreating, taking normal levels of action (what most people do), and taking massive action (what the truly accomplished people are willing to do).
- Nothing worthwhile in life comes by accident, but by taking action. The greater the action you take, the bigger the chances of success. Take average action, you get average results. Take responsibility for your goals and consistently choose to do more than the average person will. Take massive action and psychologically resign yourself to the fact of hard work.
- One reason for self-sabotage is resistance—the negative thought

patterns, blind spots, low self-esteem, self-biases, laziness, and plain old fear that keep us unable to act. But you are not your resistance.

- Either wage war against your resistance or befriend it and gratefully listen to what insights it has to share. Either way, take charge of your process and keep taking action no matter what.

Part 3: Learning to Say Yes, Learning to Say No

Chapter 6: One Trick to Double Your Chance of Success: Implementation Intention

What makes some people better able to stick to their goals and implement new habits while other people fail to do so? You might wonder if it's self-discipline, intelligence, grit, motivation . . . but actually it might be none of these things.

A study published in the *British Journal of Health Psychology* had researchers asking 248 people to try to build a new exercise habit over a period of two weeks. People were divided into three groups; the first was the control group, and they were simply asked to track their exercise frequency. The second group was the motivation group, who was asked to track their frequency but also watch a presentation about the health benefits of exercise. The third group also watched the presentation but was asked to make a plan for **when** and **where** they would exercise in the coming week. They completed the sentence:

"During the next week, I will partake in at least twenty minutes of vigorous exercise on [DAY] at [TIME] in [PLACE]."

Can you guess how each group did? Up to thirty-eight percent of group one exercised at least once per week. Interestingly, the second group showed similar levels (the presentation clearly had no impact!). The third group exercised on average at least twice a week—double the frequency of anyone else. In other words, simply writing down in black and white the when and where of their intention made group three participants reach their intention at twice the rate of groups who didn't. Reading or hearing about the benefits of exercise meant nothing (i.e., "motivation")—it was purposefully stating your intention for where and when that made the difference.

The sentence the researchers asked group three to create is called an *implementation intention.* **It's simply a plan you make beforehand about when and where you will act, or how you intend to implement a certain habit.** It works because human habitual behavior is often triggered by certain cues. For example, whenever we find ourselves in a movie theater, we suddenly feel like eating popcorn. The most powerful cues are often time and place cues. If you set an implantation intention, you are harnessing the time and place and telling yourself that when a certain situation arises, you will act in some pre-determined way. It's an "if X, then Y" conditional statement.

It doesn't matter what the action is or what habit you are trying to build; being clear about how you'll behave makes it more likely that you will behave that way when the time and place come to be. **Follow-through, then, is not a question of discipline or willpower, but simple a concrete and clear *intention* to do so.**

This means that if you have an intention, it will more likely come to be if you can be specific and say exactly what you will do, and when and where. Instead of "I'm going to eat better," you could say "I'm going to have a green smoothie every morning for breakfast in my kitchen at 7 a.m." Other examples:

- I will journal for five minutes before I sleep every evening at 10 p.m.
- I will work on my novel in my bedroom before school every day.
- I will walk for one hour at 5 p.m. when I'm done with work and before dinner.

It's not rocket science—when you hold an intention without a plan for how that intention will be implemented, it never becomes more than an idle wish. When will it happen? "Someday." Maybe we imagine that inspiration will strike at some point in the future, or that at some indeterminate point later on, we will suddenly know what to do and how. But again, thinking about action is not the same as action. Until we actually act, nothing has realistically changed for us.

What if you don't follow through?

It happens. This technique will make your new habit more likely to occur, but it's not guaranteed to occur by any means. But here, you can use conditional statements to work with your real life as it actually unfolds. So let's say your intention is: *I will walk for one hour at 5 p.m. when I'm done with work and before dinner.* But then one day work runs late due to factors beyond your control, and when you knock off at 5:45 p.m., it's raining heavily. You're already feeling a cold coming on, so you decide not to walk in the rain and potentially make yourself sick. However, you've already given this exact scenario some thought. When you made your first intention, you added a second part to it: *If I can't walk outside for whatever reason, I will do an equivalent indoor walking workout instead at home in the living room.*

Unexpected situations will always crop up, but that doesn't mean you can't build in some fail-safes. If you don't manage to work on your novel one day, you do an extra five minutes the following day. If you don't journal for five minutes one evening, you decide to spend some time meditating and doing breathing exercises instead. You are still stating your intention, but not allowing snags and setbacks to derail you. Sure, you cannot control these things completely, but that doesn't mean you have to be a complete victim to them, either. As always, keep your focus on *action* and what you can practically do in every moment to bring you closer to what matters.

You Don't Need Willpower, Just a Plan

If you don't set up an intention in this way, then what you are doing is forcing yourself to rely on something a lot flimsier: fleeting motivation and inspiration in the moment. And if *that* was reliable at all, then we would all have no problem achieving our dreams and goals, right?

Without a plan, you are asking too much of yourself. The way your life is currently set up right now is comfortable and easy—it will take effort to break up that momentum, go against your environment, and do something different. But if you set up your intention in the way described above, you are using that same environment to help you enact new behavior since times and places can act as triggers.

It is very difficult to do something from pure motivation alone, but far easier to

do it because your environment has reminded you to.

How to Use Implementation Intentions to ACT

Let's take a closer look; this technique works best when you are consciously and intelligently linking up environmental cues with goal-directed responses that you have already identified as valuable. This can be done in roughly three steps:

Step 1: Choose a goal

Step 2: Think about a path to the goal and potential obstacles on that path

Step 3: Create an if-then plan that will hook onto a cue that genuinely exists in your world

For Step 1, you need to have a goal or intention. The clearer, stronger, and simpler this is, the better. You may never have actually had to stop and formulate what this goal really is, but now is the time to get crystal clear about it. Let's say your goal is to lose weight (a very common goal!).

But this is still as yet not a well-formulated goal, primarily because it focuses only on the outcome, which you are not strictly in control of. Instead, try to rewrite the goal in terms of habits.

What *behaviors* would you like to implement that lead to or create this goal? For example:

"I will walk ten thousand steps a day."

"I will skip breakfast every morning."

"I will go to the gym three times every week."

That's why for Step 2, you have to decide on the *behavioral path* that will take you to this goal. Only you know what your strengths and limitations are, what your daily schedule looks like, what will likely work and what won't "take." Only you know what daily ritual is most likely to take root, as well as what habits are already in place that might help or hinder that new ritual.

Let's say you want to walk ten thousand steps every day. Let's say you also know that you work a busy office job and work really hard during the day, leaving you little time to go for leisurely walks. So you break up the ten thousand steps and make sure you get off the subway one stop earlier in the morning so you can walk the rest of the way to work, do the same on the way home in the evenings, plus commit to walking an additional half hour over your lunchbreak.

This leads neatly into Step 3, which is where you put these "if-then" plans into practice. Find a situational cue for the first "if" part, and then connect it to the desired behavior. For example:

"If it's 6:30 a.m. or earlier and I'm on the subway, then I'll get off at the X stop and walk the rest of the way to work."

"If it's 5 p.m. and I'm going home, I'll get off at the Y stop and walk the rest of the way home."

"If it's lunchtime, I'll walk for thirty minutes in the park before getting a sandwich."

Now, an optional extra thing you can do is identify potential obstacles and create an if-then intentional behavior in the event that things don't go according to plan:

"If I'm too late in the mornings to walk before work, I'll get my sandwich to go and walk for an hour at lunchtime instead of thirty minutes."

"If it's too dark or rainy to walk after work in the evenings, I'll do a twenty-minute YouTube workout when I get home."

A few things to keep in mind:

- Try to think of your new behaviors as "hooking" on to existing behaviors and cues. For example, if you want to consistently take a new vitamin, schedule it after you brush your teeth every day. You already brush your teeth every day without thinking of it, so "piggybacking" this new habit onto the old one requires no additional memory, motivation, or willpower. Just set the intention: "If I brush my teeth, then I take my vitamin."
- Make most of your triggers ones of place and time—preferably places you attend daily!
- Don't forget to make "contingency" plans for when your original trigger fails or isn't present. That way, even *not* following a trigger is itself a trigger.

- Try to always think of your goals in terms of habits and repeatable actions (like cycling to work instead of driving), rather than grand outcomes (such as losing weight). "Losing weight" is vague and doesn't translate to *action*, even if you have a very clear idea of how much weight to lose. But it's always very clear to see whether you have cycled to work or not!

Chapter 7: Make a NOT-To-Do List

Are you one of those people who has a firmly entrenched to-do list habit? This way of doing things is so automatic for many of us that we never really stop to question the underlying premise: If you have a few tasks to accomplish, doesn't it make sense to make a list of them and work your way through systematically?

The thing is, "action" isn't just about what you get done. Yes, you want to make sure that you know what is important and that you're spending most of your time on the things that are. "Action," then, is also about what you consciously choose **not** to do. Whenever you have a priority and say, "This is important," you are simultaneously saying, "And that means this other thing is not as important."

A to-do list can be an essential part of organizing and planning your day ... or it can be a time-sink and a distraction. A to-do list fails when it tricks you into thinking that there is value in being busy no matter what that busyness is. You feel like a million things are competing for your attention, and you get the thrill of thinking that you are hard at work ticking off all those things as you work your way down the list.

But how many of those tasks are genuinely adding value? How many of those tasks brought you demonstrably closer to your goals?

Good decision-making is elegant decision-making—it's something we do with purpose, clarity, and strategy (we'll look more closely at this in a later chapter). A to-do list is a mini schedule of tasks we've decided we need to do that day. However, if we haven't properly thought through why we need to do those tasks and in what order of priority, then we risk wasting time with useless "busy work."

Enter the not-to-do list. This contains all those tasks that you might be tempted to waste time with but shouldn't. Things that you can comfortably eliminate from your life forever with no real loss of value. What kinds of things go on the list? Here are some ideas:

- All those things you've already said no to and placed a boundary against
- Things that you know are addictive and distracting (social media, for example)
- Other people's responsibilities and obligations
- Things that don't add anything to life and don't strictly need to be done at all
- Bad habits
- Tasks or activities that are actively harmful to you
- Things that are *a tiny bit* useful but get in the way of more impactful tasks that should come first

Think about the last to-do list you made. How many items did you note down? If you had a sprawling list of twelve tasks, chances are that many of them simply should not have been there. The saying goes "if you have more than one priority, then you don't have any priorities." Granted, average people do tend to have more than one thing on their to-do list, but it's worth reminding yourself that if *everything* on your list seems "urgent," you have a priority problem.

Decide What You DON'T Care About

None of us have infinite resources. None of us will live forever, and given that there is only so much time and energy, we have to choose which paths in life we want to walk down, and which we are happy to leave unexplored. You might think that you automatically know what you don't prioritize, but then an unexpected task might emerge to derail you, and you'll get confused and waste time on it. Our resources may be limited, but our environments tend to be full of never-ending demands and distractions. Unless we consciously say NO to these things, they threaten to divert our efforts to something that matters far less to us.

Step 1: Dedicate some time

Devote thirty to sixty minutes thinking about what *isn't* your priority, and you may very well save yourself hours of wasted time later down the line. Consider it an investment in yourself.

Step 2: Look at old to-do lists

Begin your list by considering how you've organized yourself in the past. In the previous month, what did your lists look like? What tasks recurred most often? Go back through your calendar or diary and look for patterns. See if you can see any themes emerging in the demands and requests made on you, and how often you were able to tick everything off your list.

Step 3: Pick tasks to eliminate

Now start compiling a list of tasks you really don't need to do, inspired by what you learned in Step 2. For example, if you notice that approximately once a week, you end up picking up your colleague's slack and find yourself rushing to sort out their emergency at the expense of your own schedule, then this needs to change. "Colleague's work" should go on your not-to-do list.

Likewise, you may see that you are routinely getting stressed and unhappy with the task "meditate twenty minutes." This task seems to float forever on your to-do list, always seeming like the last outstanding chore and something you invariably put off till tomorrow. You feel guilty and annoyed every time you see it there. What's happening? Why is it not working? You put on your not-to-do list the following item: "Any new habit that I haven't actively committed time and space to." Either you deliberately carve out a time and place where you will meditate, or you simply don't put it on the list to haunt you and make you feel bad. Maybe in a few weeks you discover that this meditation item was dead weight and simply something you thought you should do but never made any concrete plans to do so and (being honest) won't derive much benefit from. Time to let it go!

As you look at the preceding month (or longer, if possible), ask yourself some of the following questions:

How much value is this task really adding?

Does the task have a direct link to my stated goals?

How do I feel doing this task? How do I feel seeing the task on the list?

Is this task taking time, attention, or other resources away from something more important?

Is the task something I should never have been doing in the first place?

What am I routinely unable to tick off? Why?

Have I added a task just because I like the feeling of ticking it off?

Is the task actually in my control to do anything about?

How did this task get onto my list in the first place?

This is a process that may take a little trial and error and a lot of honesty. Abandon the idea that a to-do list is always neutral and that every item on it must be completed. Not all tasks are equal, and not all uses of your time and energy will be good ones.

Step 4: Follow through with clear boundaries

When you say yes to something, you can't help saying no to something else. If you have identified one goal or dream that you really, really want, you cannot help but demote everything else to second place or eliminate it from your life entirely. This is a fact of life and never something you have to feel bad about, though!

Let's say you have put "colleague's work" on your not-to-do list. But before you know it, he has run into trouble and is asking you to pick up the slack for him again. You have to say no. Politely, clearly, kindly—but still no. The not-to-do list is not an abstract exercise; its power lies in the fact that when the time comes, you are able to turn down requests and demands that you have already identified as unnecessary or unreasonable.

It's a good idea to compile a not-to-do list once a month or so. You may need to make one more frequently if you're in the middle of a big change or transition, or if you're still ironing out some details. Armed with both a daily to-do list and a list of everything that you won't do, you have carved out a zone of action for yourself that you are confident aligns with your goals and values.

A variation on this exercise is to simply get in the habit of aggressively pruning down your to-do list. Take the pressure off.

Refocus on what matters. For example, commit to only putting three things on your to-do list every day. Just three. That may seem scary to you at first, but it also forces you to focus on what absolutely matters. Visualize the end of the day and ask what three tasks you will feel most satisfied at having completed that day. Write them down. Then tell yourself that IF you have time after these three are completed, you can do whatever you think of. But before then, don't even bother putting them on the list yet—they're just a distraction.

As you get comfortable compiling not-to-do lists, you may notice that over time they start to resemble a "life manifesto," or a collection of rules, values, and principles you hold for yourself. Here's an example of a not-to-do list that someone might compile:

- I never scroll through my phone while in bed
- I never agree to any meeting or engagement with less than twenty-four hours' notice
- I never sit down in front of my PC without a clear plan or agenda

- I never use Instagram, Twitter, TikTok, or Facebook
- I never eat after I've had my main meal for the evening
- I never allow someone to interrupt me when I'm talking
- I never make a big purchase without thinking about it for a week first
- I never do more than thirty minutes of housework at a time

As you read the above, you can probably get an idea of this person's values and priorities, right? They probably care about maintaining their health and wellbeing, keeping stress to a minimum, and living in such a way that promotes self-control and self-regulation. But look at what someone else's not-to-do list may look like:

- I never read "opinion pieces" or wild speculation
- I never ask someone's opinion about something unless they have direct experience on the topic
- I never gossip
- I never complain

- I never criticize anyone who has done their best
- I never force myself to spend time with people who are judgmental
- I never ignore a gut feeling

This person is clearly trying to live a life of integrity and positivity, and cares about tuning into their own values and intuition rather than becoming overwhelmed by other people's.

Some of your list items will be on there permanently, others just for a while as you adjust to not having a certain bad habit. It's a good idea to display your list somewhere you can see it every day. Read it often to remind yourself of what matters and what doesn't. If you do this, you might find that it ironically inspires you to action. You might be more motivated to put your foot down on behaviors that aren't working for you, or start putting limits on people, ideas, places, and activities that work against you.

Chapter 8: Find Your Priorities

If you continue to be fastidious about what you *won't* do, you might find that you naturally gravitate toward a clearer understanding of your larger life priorities. The following is a technique that keeps you organized and focused on what truly matters.

The "Burner List"

Blogger and author Jake Knapp hates to-do lists, claiming that

> "Most to-dos are just reactions to other people's priorities, not mine. And no matter how many tasks I finish, I'm never done—more to-dos

are always waiting to take their place. To-do lists just perpetuate the feeling of "unfinishedness" that dogs modern life."

However, he also feels like they're a necessary evil and still uses them. After much trial and error, he created his own system called the "burner list." The method is simple. First, gather a pen and paper, and with the paper in portrait orientation, make two tall columns:

- The left column is for the "front burner"
- The right column is for the "back burner"

Imagine that this is a cooker top with four burners in your kitchen. The front burner, the left-hand column, is where your single most important project is listed. Importantly, this is just ONE priority, no more. Write down this task in the top left quadrant, and then you can list the separate, smaller tasks needed to address it below.

Knapp recommends also keeping some "counter space" in the lower left quadrant, below your priority. This space is simply there for when you need to add more tasks to the main priority. But just like in a real kitchen, the goal is not to fill up your counters—it's to keep them clear for when you need the workspace.

The back burner, i.e., the right-hand column, is for your second most important task. List out the tasks you need to tackle this in the same way you did for the front burner. What about the lower right quadrant? Well, that's for everything else—the "kitchen sink." This is for any miscellaneous tasks or items that don't belong to either your first or second most important projects. This means that, yes, even if you have two or three more "important projects," they go into the kitchen sink with everything else if they are less important than project one and project two.

In a kitchen, the cook will always focus on the most important dish on the front burner. He doesn't completely ignore what's on the back burner, but he has a very clear idea of what gets his focus at any one moment. There's no guilt or confusion or angst over focusing on the priority, either. This method is intentionally simplified to force you to prioritize. According to Knapp, nobody ever needs more than one priority to focus on, with a strong secondary project. Everything else can wait!

Knapp also explains how he will have a current list that he will scribble on over the course of a few days, but that the list is frequently discarded once it has served its purpose. Trying this method yourself, you may find that the items in the kitchen sink can often be ignored, delegated, or paused indefinitely. At the same time, as you complete tasks on the front burner, you can start to add more things—perhaps move something from the back burner to the front, or consider the items in the kitchen sink. But do this *only* when the front burner is cleared.

The burner list is about developing the discipline to focus on one priority at a time. But it's also about training yourself to see this focus as normal and acceptable—even desirable. Too many of us have complicated, overloaded to-do lists that we don't clear, and every uncompleted action fills us with dread, guilt, shame, and resentment. It shouldn't be that way. Create your burner list and mentally tell yourself that the things in the kitchen sink are just not that important.

Warren Buffett's 5/25 rule

Now being in his nineties, Warren Buffet, "the Oracle of Omaha" and the world's fifth richest man, is not just a master investor, but admired for his business acumen and philosophy around productivity. In fact, his 5/25 rule is one such example of his much respected wisdom for how to achieve the most you possibly can with the sources and time you have available.

Buffett wanted to figure out how to prioritize and focus on the goals he really cared about (in his case, that was making a lot of money!) when so much else was demanding his attention. He knew that **if there are too many goals or distractions, it's easy to lose focus, get tired or confused, and worst of all, fritter away limited resources till they become ineffectual.** To address this, Buffett devised a simple three-step rule he would end up using himself. The steps are straightforward:

1. Make a list of your top twenty-five career goals (or, if you like, more general life goals)
2. Go through the list and circle only the five that truly speak to you.
3. Cross off the other twenty

Sounds simple, right? The thing is, while most of us already know that it's important to have priorities, in reality what ends up happening is that we keep generating new goals . . . without quite achieving the previous ones or ever taking the time to update or reassess any of them. We know that the first step is to *make* the goals. Then we fall off the wagon, lose motivation, or fail to muster the discipline to follow through. So we start again, perhaps adding another goal to the list. In this way, we start to lose clarity and focus.

While the burner list is a more "granulated" technique we can use every day to help us plan the smaller tasks, Buffett's 5/25 rule can help you identify the bigger goals that you're working toward in this way. In fact, many productivity gurus actually think that five goals is on the ambitious side, and choose to focus on *just one*. That doesn't mean they only care about one thing in life, but it does mean that, for the time being, that important goal is going to take the majority of their attention.

Now, here is where the technique gets a little unusual. The technique supposedly came about after Buffett gave airline pilot Mike Flint some advice on how to achieve all the things he wanted to in life. Buffett advised him to follow the three steps above, but supposedly the purpose wasn't to identify a list to focus on, but rather to take a close look at the twenty items on the "B list" and truly grasp how **these were the problem**. These are the things that drain away limited time and resources and keep you from fully investing yourself in the five most important items on the "A list."

Again, Buffett drives home the idea that when it comes to achieving anything of significance, it's not just what you do that matters, but what you don't do. The tricky thing is that the twenty B-list goals you list actually are important to you. On the surface they definitely look like worthwhile things—for example, completing a course, tackling a new DIY project at home, learning a new skill, taking up a new language, or earning a specialist certificate in your line of work. None of these things is bad in the least... but they will distract you all the same.

Buffett's technique asks you to shift the way you look at goals. Typically, people will decide that a goal is worth pursuing just because it sounds like a good idea. It speaks to their values; they believe they "should" do it for whatever reason, and that's that. But what they fail to do in that process is consider how this goal compares *relative to other things that are also important.* The world is full of important and interesting-sounding goals. You need to be crystal clear about which of them you nevertheless won't have time or energy for.

Consider the example of a well-accomplished, energetic CEO who thrives on hard work, goal-setting, and constant personal development. For such a person, setting goals is like breathing—they love having something to work toward, and when there's a goal on the horizon, it brings purpose and drive and excitement to life.

But you can guess where this is going. When asked to list their goals, this person can easily rattle off a list of dozens of commendable projects. They want it all: to be top of the game at work, to be the world's most perfect spouse, to raise superhuman kids, to be fulfilled creatively, to have a finely honed physique that a bodybuilder would envy, and to find time to walk the dog every single day, no excuses.

There's nothing wrong with any one of these goals, and each of them will bring fulfilment once achieved. The trouble is that there are just too many!

So the CEO spreads themselves thin over all these many goals, indeed adding goals before previous ones have been achieved. The result is predictable: They're stressed at work, they're a distracted and irritable spouse, they're an absent parent, they have been putting off their creative project for months, and they've gained a few pounds to boot. Maybe they manage to walk the dog here and there, though. Where did all their energy and drive go? Somehow, in being divided up across all the dozens of goals, it was reduced to nothing. They've multitasked in the sense that *all* their jobs have been approached with the same level of carelessness and 122ediocreity.

With Buffett's technique, the idea is to gain focus by *ranking* goals, not by considering their absolute value. If you were to look at someone else's list of twenty-five items, for example, you would not be able to say that five of them were "good" and twenty were "bad"—they would all look pretty good. But just because a goal would be nice to achieve, and just because someone else has chosen that particular goal, doesn't mean that it has to be your goal. By the same token, even if it is one of your goals, it doesn't automatically make it a *priority*.

Buffett's technique is a constant reminder that we can't do it all. There *will* be some worthwhile avenues of exploration that we have to forfeit. There will be some great goals that would be wonderful to achieve. But you need to ask "Do I want to achieve this goal at the expense of this other one I've also identified?"

When it comes down to it, your ability to meet a goal requires the ultra-pragmatic realization that some of your desires will need to go unmet. If you're an ambitious Type A person, this can actually be a hard pill to swallow. But rest assured, choosing fewer goals make you *more* effective and *more* focused so that you ultimately achieve *more*. Could you imagine yourself doing twenty-five full-time jobs? Probably not! In the same way, don't try to give yourself twenty-five life goals.

Buffett said:

"The difference between successful people and really successful people is that really successful people say no to almost everything."

Be ruthless. Keep on appraising what matters the most. Make peace with the fact that your time on earth is limited, and so are your resources. There are no two ways around it: This means you have to choose. When something comes along to demand your time, energy, or attention, remind yourself that it is a DISTRACTION. Every second you spend on it is a second that didn't go to the goal that matters most. It's a waste.

If you find yourself repeatedly drawn to the B list, stop immediately and ask what task you can do right away toward something on your A list. In extreme situations, you might want to reconsider what is on the A list. But then realize it's a trade-off—you only have five spots on the A list, so whatever you want to pursue from the B list has to come at the expense of something on the A list. Literally seeing this compromise in black-and-white can drive home the point and remind you what's at stake.

Adopt a minimalist, calm, and focused approach. Simply refuse to be distracted by the endless noise "out there" in the world—especially when it comes to other people's goals or the things that society has told you to want. Keep asking yourself: **would I rather make real and genuine progress in a single goal that actually means something to me, or muddle along in mediocrity with a thousand little goals that don't amount to anything all together?**

The choice should become much clearer then!

Summary:

- Research shows that writing down *when* and *where* you intend to implement a behavior ("an implementation intention") dramatically increases your chances of following through. Make clear if-then statements but also build in fail-safes—further implementation intentions—for when life doesn't go to plan.
- Choose a goal, think about a path to the goal and potential obstacles on that path, then create an if-then plan that will hook on to a cue that genuinely exists in your environment.
- You're more likely to succeed if you have clarity around your priorities. Make a not-to-do list for those tasks that you might be tempted to waste time with but shouldn't. Spend some time identifying tasks to eliminate, and then follow through with firm boundaries. Be ruthless about

anything that is not adding value or bringing you closer to your goals. Eventually, your not-to-do list will resemble a personal values manifesto.
- Try a "burner list" to identify the biggest and second biggest priority, and put everything else in the "kitchen sink" for later, when your most important tasks are done. Get used to ignoring things that are unessential without guilt or distraction.
- Warren Buffett's 5/25 rule can also help you identify priorities by showing you what to "avoid at all costs"—those secondary goals that only take resources away from more important ones. Don't fritter away resources; ask about a goal's relative, not absolute value, and choose only the five that matter most, avoiding the others at all costs. Rank goals and be hyper-focused on only the top ones.

Part 4: Getting Organized

Chapter 9: Simplify Your Decision-Making with a Superstructure Method

Sometimes, it's pretty obvious what you need to do. For example, you don't have any clean clothes, so there's no question that you have to do the laundry.

Other times, you are facing a big life decision that requires time, thought, and reflection. Maybe you need to decide whether to get divorced, move houses, have a child, choose a degree, downsize, upsize, or make some other big, permanent change to the way you live your life. When things are not clear-cut, we need to contemplate possible options, weigh them, make decisions, and come to an action that is (hopefully!) the best it can be.

But there's a fact we cannot avoid: The decision-making process is *not the same as* action.

Research
Planning
Considering options
Deciding
Assessing risk
Thinking

These things all have their value, but at the end of the day, none of them is ACTION. None of them will actually carry you from where you are to where you want to be. Even worse, if we dawdle and delay too long with an inefficient decision-making process, we can start to actually undermine our chances of taking beneficial action.

For example, your team has a great new idea they want to implement, but your company immediately saddles the whole thing with pages and pages of boring and unnecessary documentation to fill out, risk assessments, meetings, and rubber-stamping. The result is that the passion for the project drains away before anything can be launched. That's because while planning and decision-making are essential, *too much* oversight and justification can stifle action and lead to a whole load of nothing.

Does this mean you have to prioritize action no matter what and just do something even when you're not sure what you're doing or why? Of course not. Rather, it's about a mindset shift where taking action is *a part of* the decision-making process. Think about the exciting new work project. Management might launch into a million different box-ticking exercises to make sure they're doing things by the book, but the truth is, beyond a certain point, they cannot predict how things will play out. There is only one way to really know if the plan will work . . . and that's to *try* it!

Your boss might say, "It's a nice idea, but I need you to do some market research first because I suspect there isn't much interest." On the other hand, she could also say, "I don't know if there's any interest. Why don't you do a free short run this weekend and see who shows up? That will allow us to gauge initial interest." In the first case, she is dealing with an unknown variable (interest levels) by continuing to plan and deliberate. In the second case, *action itself is a way to learn more about that unknown.*

Instead of guessing and trying to predict, you **test**—you try it out and see what happens. This saves you time, gets you answers, and moves things along. Whether there is or isn't any interest is beside the point—after that weekend of trying it out, you will certainly know more than you did if you had simply waited and tried to predict interest in a hypothetical or abstract sense.

This principle of eliminating unnecessary steps and using action as a part of the decision-making process is at the heart of the superstructure method. You are not wasting time doing "research," but you are also not just blindly acting without a plan. The method is a way to bring structure and clarity to the things that ought to be a priority, making your decision-making more intelligent. Before we move on, let's consider one more crucial dimension to the method: the difference between intention, value, and cost.

Intention—why you are doing the task in the first place

Value—any benefits and positives the task will bring to your life

Cost—what you have to pay or give up to gain access to the above value

Now let's break the method down into steps and see how the process might play out when making a rather large decision, such as moving houses.

Step 1: What is your intention?

The first step is to spend some time looking at all the tasks you have on hand and to think about why you need to do these tasks at all. With something like moving house, you might find there are seemingly millions of smaller tasks. Take a deep breath and list them all out. For example:

- Update insurance policies
- Get quotes from moving companies
- Declutter garage
- Get ahold of packing supplies like boxes and bubble wrap
- Update address on driver's license
- Cancel utilities

- Have some fresh laundry and bedding ready for the new house
- Measure large furniture
- Buy new fridge
- Cancel subscriptions
- Host house-warming party
- Hire deep cleaners
- Etc.

Just doing a "brain dump" like this can help you cut down on stress and overwhelm, but it can also help you begin to clarify exactly what you're dealing with. When you can't think of anything more, go through each item and ask yourself what the point of each item is. Is the action bringing you closer to a goal of yours? There may be a few items that are actually unnecessary, or you may find a way to condense several different items into one.

When moving house, you'll be thinking about big issues like the overall lifestyle you're trying to create for yourself, your finances, and plans you have for your family. But if you're thinking about smaller issues like compiling a to-do list for the week ahead or planning a short vacation, this step will be more straightforward and take less time.

Let's say you sit down with your list and start to clarify your overall intention for this move: to do it *as quickly and painlessly as possible*. Even at this early stage, that means you can cancel the housewarming party item—that is definitely not part of your overall intention!

Step 2: What is each task's value?

Using this method, you divide the tasks and possibilities into three distinct categories:

1. Must have
2. Should have
3. Good to have

Must Have

These are the things that you absolutely cannot go without. They are necessary, and it's non-negotiable. It could be a task, idea, person, or an important raw material that you must have in order to achieve the desired results.

Should Have

"Should-haves" are also very important, but they aren't the be-all-end-all like "must-haves" are. These are all those things that fall somewhere in the middle tier, where having them would be fantastic and could have a significant impact on your results. Not having them is going to be hard, but not the end of the world.

Good to Have

These are the things that are not at all essential, but you certainly won't say no to them if they're available! They're a nice optional extra, but not pivotal. If you had unlimited resources and already had all your "must haves" and several "should haves" in place, then these extra things certainly wouldn't hurt.

Look at all the tasks you've identified and put them into one of the three categories above. By doing so, you have determined what things are your priorities (the must-haves), what things are important but less so (the should-haves), and what you can take or leave but won't say no to if there are enough resources left over (good-to-haves). You might like to rank the tasks now in their new order, clearly marking what can be avoided or ignored if necessary without it jeopardizing the value of the task.

For our example, let's say you rank some items like this (the higher rating denoting greater importance):

Must haves:
- Get quotes from moving companies (10)
- Get ahold of packing supplies like boxes and bubble wrap (9)
- Cancel utilities (10)
- Update insurance policies (8)

Should haves:
- Update address on driver's license (7)
- Measure large furniture (7)
- Buy new fridge (8)
- Cancel subscriptions (5)
- Hire deep cleaners (6)

Good to haves:
- Declutter garage (4)
- Have some fresh laundry and bedding ready for the new house (2)

Now, you may well look at this list and decide that you'd rank things differently—that's fine. What's important is that you take the time to clearly outline what is *essential* to the task and your overall intention.

Step 3: What does each task cost?

After determining the priority of your tasks, the next thing you should do is look at each task's cost—this includes resources like money and effort but most importantly time. Some tasks are difficult (or even impossible!), and some will require extra help from others. Some will need focused, prolonged effort and patience. If a task is nice to have but it takes hours and hours to complete, it should not be a priority. Likewise, if a task is ultra-important and it only takes two minutes to do, it makes sense to tackle it as soon as possible.

In this final step, combine the time cost of each task with its importance. How? List out all the tasks again alongside their value. Then, beside this, list out how long it will take to achieve each task. Calculate a final score by dividing the value score by the time in hours. So, for example, if getting a quote from a moving company has a value score of 10, and it takes, say, 30 minutes, its total score will be 20 (10 divided by .5 hours). On the other hand, having fresh bedding for the new house is ranked only 2 (nice to have but not essential) and will take a full 4 hours, so its score will be only 0.5.

Go through every item and divide its value by its time in hours to complete, and then order the tasks by their new score—as you can see, certain tasks will clearly emerge as more important priorities than others.

Step 4: Now schedule your tasks
If you've followed all the steps above, you'll know both the priority of each task as well as how long it will take you to complete. This means it's fairly easy to start putting everything into action. Not just any action, though—you will be systematically starting with those aspects of the project that are aligned with your intentions and have the greatest impact while demanding the least time.

You now categorically know that calling movers for a quote is what you should do next. Don't even bother getting stressed about what your housewarming party will look like, what needs to be decluttered in your garage, or whether you will have clean sheets in the new place—just focus on the things that actually matter for now.

In Step 4, we factored in the extra criterion of time to help us further rank and sort through tasks, but you may find that it makes more sense to include some other resource, such as money. You can do this by assigning each task a cost score, then multiplying that by the value score. For example, it costs nothing to phone for a quote, but a lot of money to buy a new fridge. Assign the quote task a high cost score, let's say 8, and the fridge task a low one, say 2. You will end up with scores that are now weighted according to how expensive they are, so you can first do those things that are important but cheap, and only after that consider the things that are important but expensive.

Exactly how you weigh and organize tasks is really up to you, but approaching a complex activity in this way will mean that you are always making the best of the decision-making process. Done correctly, there will be a definite end to it—after Step 4 is complete and your tasks are scheduled, you are *no longer in decision-making and planning mode, but in doing mode.* If you find yourself stressed, overwhelmed, or confused, just come back to the plan. If you find that you're distracted and stressed out one day, thinking about the exact shade of cream you'll paint the downstairs bathroom, just stop, take a deep breath, and think about it. Is this task really a priority? Is it really necessary, and have you scheduled a plan to tackle it in due course? Then, let it go and just focus on the tasks at hand. Your life will feel simpler, more streamlined, and much less stressful!

Once you have successfully ticked off all the items that are "must-haves," then you can move on to "should-haves." Finally, when you get to those tasks that are neither here nor there, you may discover with relief that they no longer even need to be done or have resolved themselves simply with the passage of time. Aren't you glad you didn't get too distracted with them or waste too much time worrying over them?

If they're still there and you *want* to do them, then great—do them. You might also decide that life's too short and instead you'd rather apply yourself to some other important task that feels more closely aligned to your values. So you forget about having a squeaky clean home the first few weeks in your new house, cut yourself some slack and decide that you don't care that much about staying on top of the laundry, after all.

The superstructure method is not perfect, but it will help you take action rather than endlessly *thinking about* taking action—and getting stressed in the process. Stop overthinking, stop waiting for permission or for the perfect time to start, and stop getting distracted with things that are not essential. **Action, it turns out, can be one of the most powerful ways of cutting through noise, fear, and inertia**. Identify what matters, then forget about everything else while you apply yourself to that task. Then repeat.

Chapter 10: David Allen's GTD—"Getting Things Done"

The acronym "getting things done" (GTD) refers to one of the most well-known and widely used personal productivity strategies out there today. The method was created by author and productivity expert David Allen, and the first edition of the book with the same title was released in 2001. After twenty years, it's reasonable to conclude that the system has stood the test of time!

If you use the GTD methodology correctly, you should find that it makes it easier for you to remain calm while working, to accomplish more, to be more creative, and to keep track of all the basics, including issues relating to both your job and your personal life.

Basically, you create a written or digital record of everything significant (such as

tasks, interests, projects, and other important data) that is currently taking up space in your head, then work through it systematically, taking action. You externalize all of this and then systematically break it down into specific, actionable work items and get to work on each, never losing sight of what your very next task is and how it fits into the bigger picture. To help you achieve this goal, Allen supplies a full set of tools, methods, tips, and techniques.

Now, the book itself is highly detailed and more than three hundred pages long. But it's possible to understand the gist of the overall system and begin to implement some of its insights right now in your own life. Naturally, Allen has the all-important "bias for action" and uses action as the ultimate benchmark for success.

GTD has five simple steps: capture, process, organize, review/reflect, and engage.

1. Capture

Our brains are better at processing information than storing it—it's just the way we've evolved. That means that we gain an advantage if we can use some sort of external data storage, i.e., keep track of everything we encounter and make sure that when we encounter something useful, it doesn't just flit away again, forgotten forever.

Building such a "second brain" frees up space and energy that you can then dedicate to higher-order intellectual, creative, or analytical tasks. Ultimately, you become more efficient, not to mention staying organized this way actually allows you to set priorities and focus, rather than just being reactive to demands and stimuli as they emerge in your environment.

So, the first step in the process is to write down everything that comes to mind. Yes, everything! This could be books or articles you want to read, questions you want answered, ideas you want to explore, chores you need to stay on top of, goals, tasks that are required on the way to those goals, exploratory ideas and concepts, notes, shopping lists, records . . . all of it needs to be captured and placed in a kind of "inbox" for processing.

Tips:

- Whenever you catch yourself having the thought "I need to, I should, I ought to," then take this as a cue that you need to capture and document there and then whatever you're thinking about. If you don't, one of two things could happen: you could have an "open loop" that hangs around and acts as a continued source of anxiety, or else you could forget entirely—and it may be a very useful thing you lose in the process.
- Create an inbox. This is any space you've set aside to hold things until you can process them. You could have a literal paper tray, a notebook, or a notetaking app that syncs across all your devices.
- Remember to handle any incoming piece of data just once—don't put it aside to deal with later. For example, if you get a notice or bill in the mail, *immediately* put it in the inbox (or throw it away if it's not relevant). Leaving it to hang around in a pile on a desk will just create a sense of unfinished business mentally, which will drain, distract, and overwhelm you.

- Don't be tempted at this stage to try to process—just capture so that you can process later.

2. Clarify

Once you've captured a bit of data, the next thing to decide is what you will do with it—the very next step. This is where the rubber hits the road. You will need to take some time where you examine everything you've captured and decide what to do with each item. At first, you need two piles: actionable and non-actionable. This is basically the question of whether you can directly *use* the information or not.

If it's **non-actionable**, you have just three options: delete, delay, or archive.
If it's **actionable**, you again have three options: defer, delegate, or do it.

Knowing that any item that you've captured can have only one of these six possible pathways goes a long way to streamlining and simplifying the accumulating mental clutter you may have in your life.

Tips:

- If something takes two minutes or less to do, do it immediately. It will not be worth your while to process and organize it; just clear it from the decks as quickly as possible and move on.
- If it takes longer than that and it's time-sensitive, clarify when and where you will act on it.
- If the item is not really a priority and not strictly your responsibility, delegate it. You may also wish to delegate it if you can see that you don't have the time or resources to do it yourself.

3. Organize

After you've clarified what each item is and done some preliminary processing, you need to organize everything. This is basically just putting things where they belong and making sure that everything required for a task's completion is stored along with it—these are "references" that provide context for each item, whether you're taking the action or assigning the task to someone else. There are four main steps to take while preparing:

1. Put an item in four of the main action lists (projects, next action, waiting for, calendar—more on this in the next section).
2. Go through each task and file it under the appropriate label.
3. Provide items with enough context. This comprises all the things you need to be able to carry out an action. This could be important background information, tools, research, contact details, etc.
4. Non-actionable items that provide some value should be stored in your archive where you can get them if they become necessary in the future. Those that provide no value at all can be deleted.

4. Reflect

You reflect in order to check that everything is up to date. The value of a high-quality productivity system declines if it is not kept current and well maintained—like a tree that needs constant pruning. In fact, an out-of-date system can be a source of stress rather than a solution for it.

Reflection can be done without judgment or negative feeling—simply observe what necessary changes and adjustments you need to make to your list, your workflow, and your results. This can be done daily when you're just starting out, or less frequently once you get in the swing of things. Look at your overall schedule and work routine and be curious about what is and isn't working. You could, for example, take five to ten minutes at the start of every day to

- Check your calendar
- Look at your next-action list and prioritize some tasks from there
- Empty your inbox
- Reference other lists as needed

Remember that the system is a living, breathing thing that is constantly changing. Regularly go in to tie up loose ends and review.

5. Engage

You're in the flow of taking notes, getting things organized, making lists, and checking in with yourself to see how you're doing.

Eventually, though, you need to do just one obvious thing: act.
In engaging, there are two priority frameworks for making decisions.

The four-criteria model is how you can make intuitive decisions about what comes next. You choose to act in the moment based on the following criteria, in order:

- **Context**—At any point in time, you can only do what you are capable of doing, given the constraints of your environment.

- **Time available**—In his book *The Effective Executive*, Peter Drucker explains that many small increments of time are essentially no time at all. Effective people merge their time into large chunks as much as possible. This allows them to really get into a flow state and get important work done.

- **Energy available**—After taking time and context into account, choose what to do next based on how much energy you have. Your energy and focus naturally diminish as the day progresses, so you might as well have an inventory of low-level menial tasks that can be done during your lowest energy ebbs.

- **Priority**—The final criteria for making decisions about what to do next boils down to priority. Of all the things you *could* do, what *should* you do?

The Threefold Model for Evaluating Daily Work

This is the second paradigm for considering how to approach one's task. At any one time, you are engaged in one of three sorts of activities:

1. Defining your work
2. Doing predefined work
3. Doing work as it shows up (i.e., being reactive rather than proactive)

If you do the GTD protocol correctly, you should only be engaging with 1 and 2, and never 3. You define your work when you process your inbox. You complete predetermined tasks whenever you carry out the tasks on your next-action lists. If you are finding yourself distracted with tasks that have not been defined or prepared for, then you are in a kind of reactive mode, and this is a sign to tighten up your process, find your priorities, or be more ruthless with how you spend your resources.

So, those are the basics. As you can probably see, the overall process is designed to simplify life and make it less stressful, even though it at first may seem to be rather complicated. Nevertheless, it's always possible to take elements from the system and apply them to your life, even if the full framework is not applicable. What's important is that the system should allow you to spend less time on stress and busywork and more time on, well, getting things done. Your goal should be to create less of a mental burden, not more.

Now that you've got a sense of the overall flow of the five steps, let's take a closer look.

Action Lists

In Step 3, you got to work organizing your items into groups, i.e., action lists:

- **Do immediately**—for tasks that take less than two minutes to complete.
- The **next-action** list—the main task list, where each item is provided with context.
- **Project planning**—if any item takes more than two steps to complete, then you need to have a plan for how to do those steps. Make sure that projects are broken down into smaller actionable steps.
- **Calendar**—note down all the items that you have to do on a certain date or at a certain time so you know at a glance what your day looks like.
- **Waiting-for** list—when you delegate an item and you wait for someone else to complete it.

The above are the main lists you might categorize an item into, but occasionally an item won't fit, and you may need a few extra categories:

- **Someday list**—projects you might want to do at some distant point in the future, but not focus on now. Archive for later.

- **Reference**—anything you might need at some point in the future as a reference for another task or item. This includes bookmarks, forms and documents, notes, bills, etc. Store these somewhere safe but out of the way so that they don't weigh on you as unfinished mental clutter.
- **Trash**—this is for those items that have zero actionable components, don't act as reference for anything, and bring no value. Get rid of them as soon as possible or else they threaten your peace of mind and workflow!

As you make your action lists, remember to categorize things according to their priority, the context, the time and energy you have available, and so on.

Now, you might look at all the above and feel immediately overwhelmed. Surely not everyone has enough time in their lives for this much organizational detail? Relax—the model is comprehensive framework, but again you don't need to use all of it. In fact, you may already be implementing various parts of it in your life without knowing it.

An Example

The best way to really understand Allen's GTD system is to see it in play—preferably in your own life! But an example can also illustrate how the program is about creating a workable flow of tasks that minimize stress while maximizing your action and output.

Let's say you run a business that does the bulk of its selling online. Let's say you are already well-versed in the GTD protocol and have streamlined your process. You start your day at 8:30, and the first thing you do to get going is look at your calendar. You have two main projects on the go at the moment (akin to front and back burner projects): sourcing a new supplier for one of your products, and revamping the website with some updated content. The former is your biggest priority for this week.

You then check your email; you *immediately* (it takes less than two minutes) clear away junk mail and spam (blocking them for the future), and while you're at it, you process your physical mail this way too. There is one interesting item in the mail, though: an advertisement. You're not interested in the product, but the ad gives you an idea for a blog post. You immediately put this in a folder you have reserved specifically for ideas of this kind. You make a note on your project list to mention this ad to your marketing person when you have a meeting with them in two days' time. Now your email inbox is clear, and there is zero mail on your desk—what you haven't acted on goes into the trash. You experience calm and composure.

Just then someone calls you and asks a tricky question about refunds that came from the team doing your web hosting. This is definitely important and a priority, but you realize that you can't deal with it just at that moment because you have an important meeting in five minutes (the meeting is about the new supplier—so it takes priority). You either delegate the task to the person calling, or ask them to defer it for two hours, when you have time and resources to address it.

It's two minutes before the meeting and you get another call . . . this time from a friendly sounding woman who wants to tell you about a charitable foundation that is doing work in your field, asking if you'd be interested in a collaboration happening sometime in the next year. Though it seems fascinating and you are interested, there's not really any rush to act. You are polite but agree to call her in a month. You quickly schedule in a reminder and make a note in your "someday" file to research the foundation and their work. Once you've scheduled all this in your elaborate "second brain," you forget about it completely. When your meeting rolls around, your head is clear, calm, and collected. There is absolutely nothing lingering from the preceding hour to distract, overload, or stress you, and nothing to impede your optimal performance in that meeting.

As you can see, the GTD system is a *way* of doing things rather than a distinct set of tools or techniques. It's about HOW more than it is about WHAT. There is a lot more to Allen's system, and many people have made their own tweaks and adjustments as necessary. There will be a time of trial and error as you figure out how best to apply the system to your own unique life. But once the system is up and running, it will allow your life to flow with a smoothness and sense of calm that is well worth the initial effort.

- Make sure you don't have open loops—grab ahold of things, act on them, or make a plan to act on them. The world is not an overwhelming or confusing place—but the way we deal with it can make it seem so!
- If you're feeling anxious, overwhelmed, or confused, take this as a cue to remind yourself of your desired outcome (your priority) and the very next step toward that. Tune everything else out.
- Always give yourself plenty of time to plan, analyze, sort, and prepare. This is a valuable investment in yourself and should not be squeezed in around tasks or done with a sense of guilt. Identify snags and move past them quickly without getting bogged down in negative feelings about them.
- Never "juggle." If there is a lot on your plate, cut through what is inessential and put the rest into some kind of organization. There is no point stressing over something—deal with it or get rid of it, then give yourself permission to move on.
- Finally, it only works if it works for you. If you try in good faith to use a tool

or method and it really doesn't work for you, it's okay to drop it. Each of us has different obligations, personalities, and lifestyles; find the level of complexity and detail that works for you and go for it.

Summary:

- To make better decisions, try to always remember that the decision-making process is *not the same as* action. Never get distracted by the organizing process, and constantly return to action. The superstructure method distinguishes between our intention behind a task, the value of the task, and what it will cost to access the task's value.
- First, do a brain dump of all the tasks you need to do, then carefully work through to assign each task a value—is it must have, should have, or good to have? Next, decide how much time, resources, or energy each task will cost you, then allow this to guide you as you schedule each item.
- Action is a powerful way of cutting through noise, fear, and inertia. Identify what matters, forget about

everything else, and apply yourself to the most important task. Then repeat.
- David Allen's GTD protocol—Get Things Done—is a comprehensive system for boosting your productivity and organization while lowering stress, distraction, and overwhelm. Create a written or digital record of everything significant and store it externally in a "second brain." Then categorize each item so that you can work through it systematically, transforming it with action.
- GTD has five simple steps: capture, process, organize, review/reflect, and engage. When making action lists, carefully consider the context, the time and resources available, and the priority level. Spend time defining your work and actually doing it, and much less time being merely reactive to things that show up.

Part 5: Overcoming the Roadblocks

Chapter 11: How to Use the Character Alarms Method

Imagine a twenty-something student who has just earned a coveted spot on a difficult graduate program. They are smart, driven, and passionate, but within a few months, they start to seriously suspect that their place in the program was just some kind of wild fluke. They look at the other students and feel inferior—could the admissions team have made a mistake letting them in? While they assume that all the other students are comfortable and finding the work easy, they feel as though they don't truly deserve to be there, they don't belong, and it's only a matter of time before they are found out to be a complete fraud . . .

Consequently this student finds themselves procrastinating more and more, skipping class or brushing off their success. **You might recognize this crushing feeling as "imposter syndrome," and indeed it can be a major impediment to taking action.** If you're secretly convinced that in a way you have *already* failed (i.e., that any evidence of success is not to be trusted), then of course you would be reluctant to take action and prove to everyone just how inferior you are. So you avoid putting yourself out there, delay the moment where you'll have to be evaluated or observed, and steadfastly run away from any challenge or competition.

The problem, of course, is that your feeling of being an imposter is completely an illusion. It's a dangerous illusion because, if it causes you to shy away from beneficial action, it may morph over time into a self-fulfilling prophesy. It's not difficult to see how. After months of procrastinating and avoiding hard work, the student in our example genuinely does find themselves performing at a lower level than others on the program who have faith in themselves.

Imposter syndrome is the result of a particular cognitive distortion that interprets everything through the lens of incompetence. Failures are exaggerated and successes are dismissed or even interpreted as additional evidence of one's lack of worth ("I got an award because they felt sorry for me"). Negative self-talk, procrastination, perfectionism, and extreme fear of failure all mean that it's especially difficult to do the one thing that you need to: take action.

There are many suggestions for overcoming imposter syndrome, but when it comes to encouraging action specifically, there is one especially good technique: the "character alarms method." The method was invented by executive coach Eric Partaker. The big idea is that you create a character who then acts as your proxy. **By embodying this character, essentially acting as though you were them, you are able to bypass all your self-limiting beliefs and get around imposter syndrome**. In a way, believing that you are an imposter is already a way of identifying with a character—only in this case, the character is an undeserving fraud!

The character alarms method counters this tendency by allowing you to see the world through the eyes of someone who isn't burdened with this self-bias. It may seem cheesy that you could just "flip the switch" and become someone else, but you may be surprised at just how easy it is to do, and how effective. Set an alarm on your phone for all those times during the day you'd like to switch on this ego. You could even set multiple alarms for many different personas, according to the kind of results you're trying to achieve in different areas of your life. For example:

You set an alarm for 9:30 in the morning, when you know you'll be in an important work meeting. This is a reminder to go into your character "The Professor." This character is a blend of people you admire for their poise and intelligence, and it's an alter ego you rely on when you need to overcome your fear of speaking up. It's what allows you to be confident in what you know, to speak up, and to carry yourself with assured confidence.

You also set an alarm for later in the day at 5 p.m., when you typically leave work. This is the point in your schedule where you most need to establish boundaries and draw a clear line between work and home life. The character you need to embody is a cross between a wise zen master and Jackie Chan—able to swiftly dispense with any unreasonable demands just as you're walking out the door or turning your inbox notifications off for the day.

Let's say your final character alarm kicks in at around 6 p.m. when you get home. Here, you embody a "domestic goddess" persona. You become a kind and attentive mother and a loving wife and play out the role of someone relishing their private sanctuary away from the chaos and noise of the outside world.

No, you are not exactly required to *pretend* to be all these different people. Rather, you are asking about the kind of actions they would take ... and then taking them yourself. While these characters are useful tools/shortcuts, they are in fact still versions of you. They're just versions that you are in the process of more actively becoming.

The idea is that the more you behave like XYZ character, the more you actually take on that identity. This argues against the beliefs we might have with imposter syndrome, i.e., thinking that nothing we do can really change who we are on a fundamental level. The character alarms technique is so powerful because it works against many of our modern assumptions. A big assumption is that our identify drives our actions. But really, the character alarms technique asks us to invert this: What is inside doesn't matter—only what you DO matters. Our actions create our identity. You have to **do** in order to **be**.

When you are trapped with imposter syndrome, you may think, "I am an incompetent/unworthy person. That's just who I am. And nothing will change that." This is why someone can continue to think they are a fraud and a failure even as they win awards and accolades. The problem is that they are focusing on *identify* and not *action*. And identity is fixed and non-negotiable. When you try the character alarms technique, you shake up these assumptions. You say, "A competent person is someone who acts in competent ways. That's what I'll do."

Your characters and alter egos are ideally only crutches that you use for the short term. Eventually, the idea is that you fuse with this alter ego and it becomes you. Ziggy Stardust, Sasha Fierce, and Slim Shady are all famous alter egos you may be familiar with—they are the inventions of David Bowie, Beyonce, and Eminem respectively. What's interesting is that these personas are often dropped after some time once they've done their job. That's because if you continue to act as the person does, eventually you *are* that persona.

We are the stories we tell about ourselves. If taking on an alter ego feels a little phony, consider that it's something you already do—except the person you may have chosen unconsciously for yourself is timid, doubtful, or self-hating. The more you act as though that "story" were true, the more it becomes true. It's a little quirk of our brains that the more we are exposed to an idea, the more we believe it to be true. Simply seeing the same idea repeated is enough to convince us that its part of life. So, use this tendency to your advantage, and remind yourself every single day of a healthier, alternative story where you are confident, joyful, focused, and so on.

Every time you see an alarm go off, that's your cue to start seeing the world through different eyes and acting accordingly. Your brain doesn't really know what's "real" or not—it's just going along with what you think is true. Sure, the first few times the alarm goes off, you may feel like you're being fake and a little bit silly. But after a while, you may find that you are not really playing a part anymore. You are genuinely teaching yourself to respond to stimuli in a different way and to make different choices.

The more you do this, the more you will realize that your "real" self was probably just fiction, anyway. Do you think that your old conception of who you are is the more accurate one just because it's the least flattering? Strange how that happens, isn't it! Become curious about that moment you decided that the voice telling you that you were an awesome person was "silly" and "pretending," while the voice that told you that you were a useless failure was "real" and "the truth."

Chapter 12: Beat Procrastination with Microtasks

Do you suffer from procrastination?

The first thing is not to panic—it's very, *very* normal!

You've probably heard that the best way to beat procrastination is to "just start" with a small task and go from there. This is excellent advice—but it also tends to work mostly for tasks that are less complex. If you're putting off cleaning the kitchen, for example, this approach will help you gather momentum and break out of that stagnant state of inaction. But there are tasks that are more complex and intimidating than cleaning the kitchen, and for this you'll need a more defined strategy—such as using "microtasks."

Self-help guru Steve Pavlina suggests that you break down your *entire* project into microtasks first, from the start to the very end, before taking any action. What counts as a microtask? That's easy: anything that cannot reasonably be broken down any further. These tasks are usually ten to twenty minutes long and have a definite moment that you can identify as a natural stopping point. Part of the value of microtasks is also that they are arranged in sequence, i.e., in a plan that essentially outlines a step-by-step approach for how to tackle any task.

When you are compiling such a list of microtasks, keep focused by narrowing in on just one verb per item. Verbs matter because they're action words—they tell you exactly what you're doing. Sometimes, progress on a task can stall because you have only the vaguest idea of what you're actually supposed to be doing, or you have ill-defined items on your to-do list, like "think about vacation" or "sort out bathroom cupboards." What does "sort out" really mean? And how

will you know when you have thought about
your vacation enough and can tick this item
off the list?

**As you make your list of microtasks, focus
on each item's single objective.** Just the act
of writing everything down may help you
break some tasks down or combine several
smaller ones. Imagine you had the task of
arranging a going-away party for a colleague
at work. It's not a mammoth task, but it will
take some effort and the clock is ticking.

Let's say you know you have to "plan a
party," and this obligation hovers constantly
at the back of your mind, but you find
yourself repeatedly putting it off. Why?
Because "plan a party" is a big, complex,
difficult task. It has no clearly defined
parameters, so who even knows just how big
and stressful it is? Can you imagine sitting
down at a desk right now and "planning a
party"? Where do you start? How do you
know when you're finished?

You may sense all of this unconsciously and
decide that "plan a party" is just a boring,
difficult hassle—so you put it off. You do

what you can to avoid that knot of complexity. It's just too much.

But here's what it might look like if you were to break that all down and create a list of microtasks instead:

1. *Brainstorm* ideas for an overall theme
2. *Choose* a theme
3. *Book* a meeting room
4. *Double check* there are no major commitments for the office on a chosen afternoon
5. *Create* an invitation containing all necessary information
6. *Send* the invitation
7. *Check* budget to see what can be spent on catering
8. *Order* catering
9. *Assign* someone to set up audio equipment for some music
10. *Decide* on playlist
11. *Double-check* guests with dietary restrictions and adjust catering
12. *Assign* somebody the job of decorating venue according to theme
13. *Purchase* giant card
14. *Ensure* office has signed card

15. *Assign* someone to collect funds for gift
16. *Assign* someone to buy and wrap gift
17. *Compile* a short speech
18. *Practice* speech
19. Clear room in schedule by *delegating*, *canceling*, or *re-scheduling* tasks
20. *Ensure* you have a suitable outfit prepared

As you can see, all the verbs are in italics and emphasize the **action** necessary for each microtask to be considered complete. Run through your list at the end to make sure you have no wishy-washy items or those with verbs that are nevertheless fuzzy in their meaning. "Fix," for example, doesn't actually tell you how, and "consider" is not really an action at all.

Now, as you read your list, you might think, "This is a little uptight. Surely I don't have to be this specific and detailed?" But the magic of this process is precisely how exhaustive it is. The step-by-step process is so thorough and complete that it is **almost impossible to get stuck**—this is the goal. No matter where you are in the process, you know exactly what comes next and what you have to do to move forward. That can be a very liberating feeling!

Especially if you have a bigger project, you may end up with a very, very long list of tasks—pages long, even. That's okay. The smoother the transition between one task and the next, the less likely you are to procrastinate. That's because one of the major causes of procrastination is a lack of clarity about your process. It's a kind of mental state characterized by a stressful open-endedness. But with a microtask outline, there is no mystery. You know what you're doing and in what order and can reasonably estimate when you'll be done. If you stall or have difficulty, it's instantly clear to you what the problem is—and what you need to resolve before moving forward.

If you suffer from procrastination, it can often feel like sitting down to do your task always takes enormous effort, as though you're reinventing the wheel each time. It can feel like there is an enormous barrier to getting into the flow of things. You may find yourself unclear on what you're even doing, distracted, or feeling that there are uncertain outcomes/rewards for even those things you do manage to achieve.

A microtask list reduces that complexity and takes away much of the unknown. It introduces a level of smoothness and predictability to the process. You don't need to think of any of the big-picture questions whenever you sit down to the task, or re-face all your fears and justifications. All you have to do is sit down and proceed with the next thing on your list. The heavy lifting has already been done. It's much less overwhelming and you get the strong sense that, as long as you carefully work through one step after the other, you're on the right path and will get to where you want to be.

You might find that microtasks are almost always less intimidating than vague, ill-defined tasks. Go back and look at the microtasks for planning the party—each and every one of them is extremely easy and won't take much time. This means that "planning a party" as a task is not difficult or complex at all—but the way you approach it can make it feel that way. Trying to tackle everything at once can create a strong sense of resistance and overwhelm, and that's what leads to procrastination. Breaking things down not only takes away that intimidation factor, it also begins to outline a way froward, a direction of travel through the tasks.

When Not to Use Microtasks

This is a method that works to tackle procrastination when that procrastination is a result of overwhelm and lack of clarity. If you're facing that amorphous, complex blob of action and you're not sure how to begin, then microtasks can help you. But the technique isn't always the best approach. As already mentioned, don't bother making extensive lists of tasks if what you're dealing with is very simple, short, or straightforward. If your project is, for example, "clean the cat litter box," then taking twenty minutes to write out ten different microtasks isn't a way to counter procrastination . . . it *is* procrastination!

Similarly, a task may be pretty complex, but if this complexity is not stressing or overwhelming you, then there's little point in creating microtasks. For some people, "sort out bathroom cupboard" creates no feeling of uncertainty or anxiety, and enormous goals like "write a novel" do not lead to paralysis. Likewise, it's fine to have a bigger goal without knowing exactly how you're going to make it happen just yet. Many goals in life are iterative—i.e., you need to act, see what happens, and then go from there, adjusting your approach as you go along.

While there is nothing wrong with this, keep the microtask approach close at hand for all those moments when you need to force a degree of clarity and conciseness. At some point you need to narrow things down to small, concrete actions taken in sequence. It may be that you can only outline your tasks this way for the first week or so of a project. That's fine—make your final microtask the task of setting up microtasks when you have more information. This way, you are leaving things moderately open-ended but not allowing yourself to get too distracted or aimless on your way to the goal.

You might be wondering, "What if I create a microtask list . . . and still procrastinate?"

Well, sadly, this is not all that uncommon!

Microtask creation can *help* with the procrastination problem. But procrastination usually results from many different causes, a lack of clarity and the overwhelming size of the task being just two of them. If you create a task list and find that you're procrastinating as badly as ever, that's a pretty good sign that something else is at play:

- *Are you allowing perfectionism to make you afraid of taking action and doing things imperfectly?*
- *Are you too focused on the outcome and being too hard on yourself?*
- *Are you allowing negative self-talk, resistance, and self-sabotage to get in your way?*
- *Are you forcing yourself to do a task that is actually not possible, not relevant, or not your responsibility?*
- *Are you, quite simply, being lazy?*

This last possibility may hit a nerve for some people. Can procrastination be a complicated result of a host of psychological and behavior issues? Sure it can. It can also be a pretty predictable result of just preferring to avoid hard work. Bad habits, a lack of discipline, and an environment filled with distractions can create the conditions for putting off hard work in favor of more immediately pleasurable activities—like doing nothing. If this is the case for you, microtasks won't help much. Because no matter how small and easy you make any microtask, you can never make working on a goal more satisfying than eating candy, playing video games, or having a nap, right?

Think of the microtasks technique as a way to remove every *organizational* impediment to you taking action. Whatever remains after you've made the task as simple and easy as possible is likely down to your own lack of discipline, poor habits, or simply wanting to avoid hard work. If you still feel like procrastinating after the task is made much more manageable, then you can confidently conclude that you're being lazy. The only solution then is to push yourself.

Focus on Flow
Once you have clearly identified a path of tasks to follow, then you can focus not so much on the tasks themselves but on your state of flow. You'll know you're in a flow

state when you move seamlessly from task to task and almost don't even need to consult the microtask list because you are smoothly moving through tasks on your own steam.

The thing about being "in flow" is that it's the most efficient use of your time and energy. Switching tasks and procrastinating take more time in the long run and are more emotionally and cognitively draining than getting into a sustainable, productive workflow. In other words, doing two solid, high-quality hours on your project is more productive AND easier than stressing about it for a week, stopping and starting several times, and incurring all the emotional drama associated with quitting halfway.

The state of flow tends to kick in only after around fifteen minutes of sustained work on a task. This means that you should try to give yourself tasks that are at least fifteen minutes long, and do your best not to let yourself off the hook before this period. If you are in the habit of working for twenty-five-minute chunks, this fits comfortably—you only have to push for the first fifteen minutes, whereafter you might find yourself in the flow and able to continue. Even then, you probably only have to push on for another ten minutes before you can break, anyway. Once you're actually working, you may realize how quickly twenty-five minutes can go by . . . and how procrastination actually only draws this out and makes difficult tasks more painful!

Keeping focused is a skill. And just like any other skill, it becomes stronger with practice. Train your attention span like you train any other muscle. Every time you push through that wall of procrastination and choose action instead of inaction, you are strengthening your resolve and making it more likely you'll do the same next time.

Chapter 13: Work with Your Ultradian Rhythms

One final roadblock on the path to better productivity is one that may be harder to put your finger on. Call it tiredness, fatigue, or even burnout, but there comes a point at which we are pushing against our body's natural physiological limits.

You've probably heard of circadian rhythms, but did you know that the twenty-four-hour sleep-wake cycle is not the only one your body moves through? "Ultradian" comes from the Latin word for "outside" and "day"—it refers to all those rhythms that are shorter than the twenty-four-hour daily cycle, ranging from minutes to up to ten or twelve hours.

In this book, we have repeatedly returned to action as the fundamental point at which real change is made, and the *only* place from which to learn, achieve, and understand. While all of this is true, however, there is value in considering **when** one takes action. If you've ever tried pushing past your body's innate sense of rhythm, you already know what it feels like: near impossible. It's like trying to do a heavy workout at 2:30 in the morning—it just doesn't make sense!

Working WITH rather than AGAINST one's own rhythms is not about slacking, doing less, or giving yourself permission to be lazy. Rather, it's about consciously deciding not to make things harder for yourself than they need to be, and not choosing to make an enemy or competitor of your own body. When you optimize when you do certain actions, you preserve precious energy and get more out of the effort you do expend. This is more elegant, a lot easier, and ultimately gets more done in the long run.

In the 1950s, sleep researcher Nathaniel Kleitman found that human beings move through a sleep cycle that is roughly 90-120 minutes long, which lines up with the sleep stages of alert sleep, light sleep, REM sleep, and deep sleep. But there are cycles and stages to *waking* life, too. Kleitman called these broader waking rhythms the "basic rest-activity cycle," but today we call them ultradian rhythms, and we use them to explain why we seem to move through a 90-120-minute cycle of alertness and energy.

Generally, the ultradian rhythm is as follows: **Your body achieves a period of high alertness every 90-120 minutes. This comes in a wave and peaks before giving way to a low-energy period where you feel tired again. Then the cycle repeats.** This means that there are several times during the day when you are *naturally* more energetic and able to work, and times when you are *naturally* geared up to rest.

The idea is to simply line up your activities to fit these rhythms—don't "waste" an ultra-alert period by doing nothing, but at the same time, don't force yourself to push through what should be a rest period. During a peak energy period, you may experience challenge and demand as exciting and inspiring, and your overall state is arousal. However, when you are winding down and energy levels are dropping, these same challenges and demands might be perceived more as stress and cause you feelings of overwhelm and anxiety.

Anders Ericsson is a researcher who has been studying high performers like athletes, musicians, artists, and chess players for many years. His discovery was that the most successful people tended to train themselves in short bursts, rather than long grueling sessions without a break. His conclusion was that this was ultimately the most effective approach. Here's how you can do the same in your own life.

Tip 1: Work on your priority task for sixty to ninety minutes, no longer

No matter how important it is, do not do any single task for longer than sixty to ninety minutes at a time. Pay close attention to your body but also your cognitive resources. If you find yourself getting overwhelmed, irritable, or foggy-headed, it's not a sign of poor character or a lazy attitude—it's a sign you are moving into a rest period.

During the sixty to ninety minutes, break up your work time into smaller thirty-minute sessions, each with its own mini break. So, for example, you could practice playing the violin in the morning from 10 a.m. to 11 a.m., but at 10:25, you take a quick breather to have a drink, walk around outside, and relax for five minutes before another twenty-five-minute session at 10:30. At 11 a.m., you then take a longer break.

Tip 2: Make your longer breaks count

If you're a productivity junkie, or you're just trying really hard to get the most out of every day, it can be difficult to just *stop working* and take a meaningful break. Many of us have quite a distorted idea of what a break really is. We wrongly assume that even our breaks need to be productive somehow—perhaps we think that unless we're doing a structured mindfulness class or having a "power nap" or passively learning something while we relax, it doesn't count.

But meaningful breaks have to be just that—a break. Your brain needs to switch off completely, not just switch tasks or stress about how to relax in the most optimal way! Only you can say what will genuinely allow your brain to switch off. Go for a walk outside (not a scheduled one, just wander) or call up a friend for a conversation you really will enjoy. Yes, you can meditate if you really want to, but try not to make the whole thing a virtuous box-ticking exercise. You're not *trying* to do nothing; you really are just doing nothing.

Can't You Override Your Cycles?

Of course you can. If your life depended on it, you most likely could find a way to complete a workout at 2:30 in the morning. The problem is, doing so will trigger your fight-or-flight response and be registered by your body as an extremely stressful event. This kind of forced, unnatural action takes its toll on the body—fine for emergencies, but not sustainable in the long run if you value your health and wellbeing. Chronically ignoring your innate cycles is not a righteous thing to do; it will impair your effectiveness, ruin your health, and make your life so much more miserable than it needs to be.

Imagine that for whatever reason, you do summon up the energy to work out at 2:30 in the morning. Chances are, that workout is not going to be your best performance, and your sleep cycle, immune system, and overall mood will take a big hit. But worse than this is the fact that now you are so off-kilter that when your natural period of alertness and energy actually comes around the next morning, you are not in a position to take advantage of it!

You are exhausted and burnt out, and so miss out on that period of time where working out would have produced better results and with less effort. Why burn through reserve energy resources just to do something that you would be capable of doing easily at some other time in your schedule?

What if My Job Sets My Schedule for Me?

It's sad but true: The conventional nine to five workplace has not been set up with your wellbeing or natural rhythms in mind! Not all of us have the option of drastically rewriting our daily work schedules, but don't despair if you find that your work commitments clash with your natural patterns. There's still a lot you can do.

Most people tend to have:

- A morning peak at around 8 a.m.
- Another late-morning peak at 11:30 a.m.
- An afternoon peak at 2:30 p.m.

- A late-afternoon peak (or "dinner peak") at 5:30 p.m.
- An early evening (or "intimacy") peak just before 8 p.m.

That means that each of us has about five maximum peaks every day, but they're not all created equal—the morning and late-morning peak are the strongest, and every peak after that gets a little smaller until bedtime. Most people wake naturally at about 6 a.m., and their energy levels rise steadily until the first 8 a.m. peak. Every peak then is followed by an energy dip as follows:

- A mid-morning slump at around 10 a.m.
- A post-lunch slump just after 1 p.m.
- A late afternoon slump just after 4 p.m.
- An after-dinner slump just before 7 p.m.
- And finally a slump at about 9 p.m. that continues on into preparations for sleep

Knowing the above, you have plenty of wiggle room for how to structure your workday for maximum productivity. Even shifting some tasks by thirty minutes can make an enormous difference. There are people who have different individual rhythms, but the vast majority of human beings are more productive in the morning, so identify your most important tasks and always do them first.

Are you thinking, "Wait a second, I don't get up at 6 a.m., and I certainly don't get ready for bed at 9 p.m."? Well, understand that the above cycle has been identified as the most common *natural* cycle—i.e., one that has not been disturbed by poor sleep habits, external work demands, or anything else. It is possible that the above schedule doesn't describe your natural rhythm. On the other hand, it's also worth considering whether you might feel better and be more productive if you didn't stay up into the small hours or get only six hours of sleep every night!

When You Work, Work; When You Rest, Rest

In the post-pandemic world, more people now work at home than ever before, sometimes staying at home exclusively. Because we are all digitally connected and constantly available via devices that seem to never leave our side, it can be difficult to draw a clear line between work and rest. Having better mastery over your own ultradian rhythms is not just a question of scheduling break times every ninety minutes or so. It's also about practicing a sort of "schedule hygiene" where no rest is allowed to creep in during work hours, and no work is allowed to creep in while you're resting. Here's how to start tightening up the work/rest boundary:

- **When you're working**, especially if it's on a screen, use apps or software to prevent you from accessing distracting websites or social media. Set these on a timer.
- If a concern or worry arises, note it down somewhere and tell yourself you will engage with it later. This is called "worry postponement" and will stop you from getting derailed. Schedule ten minutes to address all the worries you've written down when you decide—you may find a lot of them have ceased to seem so urgent.

- Communicate clearly with others that you are in work mode and are not to be disturbed. Close the door, put a sign on your desk, or use some other symbol or item to signal that you are not available—be polite but firm about respecting this, and others will soon respect it, too.
- Clear desk clutter and things that could create "mental noise." Streamline and simplify so that it's easy to focus on the task at hand, and *only* that task.
- **When you are resting**, be ruthless in pushing away any demand, distraction, or obligation that poses as urgent. Unless the house is burning down, whatever it is can probably wait!
- Think not in terms of time management, but energy management. Take your task of refilling your tank with as much seriousness as you do any other task. Would you allow someone to wake you up at 2:30 a.m. to answer a routine email or look at a social media ad? If not, then don't allow that kind of thing to disturb you just because it's 2:30 p.m.

- When you are resting, do your very best not to think of what you are going to do when you stop resting. You don't have to engage in full-on Zen meditation, but if you catch yourself thinking about what's for dinner, your schedule tomorrow, or when you'll take the cat to the vet, gently stop yourself and go back to resting.

Summary:

- "Imposter syndrome" is a major impediment to taking action. It causes you to shy away from beneficial action and may morph into a self-fulfilling prophesy. This cognitive distortion can be countered using the "character alarms method." You set three alarms throughout the day to act as though you were a made-up alter ego, bypassing your self-limiting beliefs and your default focus on your own assumed incompetence.
- Our actions create our identity. You have to **do** in order to **be**. In time, you may learn to sincerely be the character you are initially only pretending to be.

- Occasional procrastination is normal and not the end of the world. Steve Pavlina suggests breaking down your entire project into ten-to-twenty-minute single objective microtasks—first, from start to finish, and then moving through each step by step. This makes your work smoother, clearer, and less intimidating.
- The microtask approach is not appropriate for small or simple tasks. Though the technique can help, it is also possible that your procrastination is down to your own lack of discipline, poor habits, or laziness.
- Bear in mind the influence of ultradian rhythms, and work with your body, not against it, when planning when to do tasks. Your body achieves a period of high alertness every 90-120 minutes before giving way to a low-energy period when you feel tired again. Plan your tasks accordingly.
- Work on your priority task for sixty to ninety minutes, no longer, and break this into smaller work cycles. Commit to creating clear boundaries between work and rest so that you are fully

focused on each without interference either way.

Summary Guide

PART 1: THE ACTION MINDSET

- There is one key feature that separates those strategies that work from those that never do: action. At some point, if you truly wish to transform your life, you will need to cross over from where you are to where you want to be—by taking action.
- To craft an action for bias, drop the belief that you need to be excellent at something the first time around, and replace it with: "Anything worth doing is worth doing poorly." Strive to be an amateur and not a professional.
- Remind yourself that all your attempts have value and that failure is valuable because it's how you learn. Abandon the need to be perfect and focus on the process of learning and growing, rather than any flashy outcome. Learn to tolerate the imperfection of being a beginner.
- Just start—"You don't have to be great to start. But you have to start to be

great." Every expert began as a newbie, so just take the first step and trust that it gets easier. Go with what works and don't allow a minor disaster to turn into a major one.
- Conventional wisdom tells us that we need motivation in order to act, but it's really the other way around: action creates motivation. Taking action breaks inertia and builds confidence and momentum—and you don't *need* to be inspired to take the first step.
- Don't wait for a perfect set of external conditions to give you permission to act. If you're feeling uninspired and unmotivated and lacking energy, the solution is a little counterintuitive: do something, even if it's small. Act from commitment, not from temporary inspiration.

PART 2: WHAT DOES SUCCESS REALLY TAKE?

- Choosing the status quo (foregoing action) is still a choice, and it comes

with risks—sometimes it's the riskiest choice. There is no way to remain in your comfort zone and grow at the same time, so learn to take strategic, conscious, and deliberate risks with the understanding that it's normal to feel fear. Fear is normal but doesn't have to be in the driver's seat.
- Be courageous not fearless; identify your goal and appraise the risks to going for it, the impact the goal will have on you, and the cost of not taking the risk. Then make a rational plan for how to mitigate those risks according to their probability of happening.
- According to Grant Cordone, there are four main levels of action: doing nothing, retreating, taking normal levels of action (what most people do), and taking massive action (what the truly accomplished people are willing to do).
- Nothing worthwhile in life comes by accident, but by taking action. The greater the action you take, the bigger the chances of success. Take average action, you get average results. Take responsibility for your goals and consistently choose to do more than the average person will. Take massive

action and psychologically resign yourself to the fact of hard work.
- One reason for self-sabotage is resistance—the negative thought patterns, blind spots, low self-esteem, self-biases, laziness, and plain old fear that keep us unable to act. But you are not your resistance.
- Either wage war against your resistance or befriend it and gratefully listen to what insights it has to share. Either way, take charge of your process and keep taking action no matter what.

PART 3: LEARNING TO SAY YES, LEARNING TO SAY NO

- Research shows that writing down *when* and *where* you intend to implement a behavior ("an implementation intention") dramatically increases your chances of following through. Make clear if-then statements but also build in fail-safes—further implementation

intentions—for when life doesn't go to plan.
- Choose a goal, think about a path to the goal and potential obstacles on that path, then create an if-then plan that will hook on to a cue that genuinely exists in your environment.
- You're more likely to succeed if you have clarity around your priorities. Make a not-to-do list for those tasks that you might be tempted to waste time with but shouldn't. Spend some time identifying tasks to eliminate, and then follow through with firm boundaries. Be ruthless about anything that is not adding value or bringing you closer to your goals. Eventually, your not-to-do list will resemble a personal values manifesto.
- Try a "burner list" to identify the biggest and second biggest priority, and put everything else in the "kitchen sink" for later, when your most important tasks are done. Get used to ignoring things that are unessential without guilt or distraction.

- Warren Buffett's 5/25 rule can also help you identify priorities by showing you what to "avoid at all costs"—those secondary goals that only take resources away from more important ones. Don't fritter away resources; ask about a goal's relative, not absolute value, and choose only the five that matter most, avoiding the others at all costs. Rank goals and be hyper-focused on only the top ones.

PART 4: GETTING ORGANIZED

- To make better decisions, try to always remember that the decision-making process is *not the same as* action. Never get distracted by the organizing process, and constantly return to action. The superstructure method distinguishes between our intention behind a task, the value of the task, and what it will cost to access the task's value.
- First, do a brain dump of all the tasks you need to do, then carefully work through to assign each task a value—

is it must have, should have, or good to have? Next, decide how much time, resources, or energy each task will cost you, then allow this to guide you as you schedule each item.
- Action is a powerful way of cutting through noise, fear, and inertia. Identify what matters, forget about everything else, and apply yourself to the most important task. Then repeat.
- David Allen's GTD protocol—Get Things Done—is a comprehensive system for boosting your productivity and organization while lowering stress, distraction, and overwhelm. Create a written or digital record of everything significant and store it externally in a "second brain." Then categorize each item so that you can work through it systematically, transforming it with action.
- GTD has five simple steps: capture, process, organize, review/reflect, and engage. When making action lists, carefully consider the context, the time and resources available, and the priority level. Spend time defining your work and actually doing it, and much less time being merely reactive to things that show up.

PART 5: OVERCOMING THE ROADBLOCKS

- "Imposter syndrome" is a major impediment to taking action. It causes you to shy away from beneficial action and may morph into a self-fulfilling prophesy. This cognitive distortion can be countered using the "character alarms method." You set three alarms throughout the day to act as though you were a made-up alter ego, bypassing your self-limiting beliefs and your default focus on your own assumed incompetence.
- Our actions create our identity. You have to **do** in order to **be**. In time, you may learn to sincerely be the character you are initially only pretending to be.
- Occasional procrastination is normal and not the end of the world. Steve Pavlina suggests breaking down your entire project into ten-to-twenty-minute single objective microtasks—first, from start to finish, and then moving through each step by step.

This makes your work smoother, clearer, and less intimidating.
- The microtask approach is not appropriate for small or simple tasks. Though the technique can help, it is also possible that your procrastination is down to your own lack of discipline, poor habits, or laziness.
- Bear in mind the influence of ultradian rhythms, and work with your body, not against it, when planning when to do tasks. Your body achieves a period of high alertness every 90-120 minutes before giving way to a low-energy period when you feel tired again. Plan your tasks accordingly.
- Work on your priority task for sixty to ninety minutes, no longer, and break this into smaller work cycles. Commit to creating clear boundaries between work and rest so that you are fully focused on each without interference either way.